W9-BPT-353

The Price Waterhouse/Euromoney International Treasury Management Handbook

Volume II: Organisation, systems and controls

Edited by
Mark Austen and Paul Reyniers

Published by Euromoney Publications

Published by
Euromoney Publications Plc,
Nestor House, Playhouse Yard,
London EC4

Copyright © Euromoney Publications, 1986

ISBN 1 870031 05 9

All rights reserved. No part of this book may be reproduced in any form or
by any means without permission from the publisher.

Printed in Great Britain by Bourne Offset Limited
2 The Ridgeway, Iver, Bucks.

Contents

List of Figures

About the editors

Mark E Austen

Mark Austen is the partner responsible for the consulting division in Price Waterhouse, London which carries out banking, financial institutions and treasury consultancy engagements in the UK. Mark also has a similar role in the PW practice in Europe for the same market sector and represents the UK and Europe on the World Firm of Price Waterhouse.

Mark joined Price Waterhouse in 1975 after gaining extensive financial control experience initially with a UK based multinational and subsequently with a merchant banking group.

Mark has worked on numerous international engagements in the private and public sectors.

Paul J Reyniers

Paul Reyniers is a partner in the consulting division of Price Waterhouse, London and is responsible for treasury management consultancy projects to the corporate and financial sector.

He joined Price Waterhouse in 1979 from the Anglo American group where he was involved in treasury, corporate finance and acquisitions.

Paul, over the last 10 years, has worked in the UK and internationally in Oslo, Luxembourg, Johannesburg and Rio de Janeiro on numerous acquisitions and projects involving corporate finance and centralised treasury management to both the corporate and banking sectors.

PREFACE

Volume II: Organisation, systems and controls

As the senior partner of the United Kingdom firm of Price Waterhouse, I am delighted to be able to present this publication to you. Our firm has now taken a lead in developing services in the treasury area geared to providing practical advice for profit improvement and risk reduction. This has been particularly well recognised in today's volatile and difficult markets.

This book is intended as a practical guide for financial directors, treasurers, financial controllers, tax specialists and commercial managers who are responsible for, manage or work closely with, the company's treasury function. It is not an academic analysis of the subject of international treasury management but specifies the infrastructure of organisation, systems and controls normally required by corporate treasurers, to manage this important corporate function.

The contents of this book have been based on the joint expertise of the consultancy, audit, international tax and international trade groups of Price Waterhouse. The materials have been based on practical experience gained by these specialist groups over the last few years, research that has been undertaken by this firm, and from discussions with treasurers of leading companies and officers of financial institutions. It is experience that has formed the foundation on which the recommended concepts and procedures set out in this book have been constructed.

The International Treasury Management Handbook consists of two volumes. Volume I addresses the key decisions on cash, funds and currency management that the treasury has to make together with the primary information flows that are required to make those decisions. This volume addresses the next level of detail to the techniques set out in Volume I and includes the organisation, systems and controls required for the treasury to function effectively.

Jeffery H Bowman
Senior Partner
Price Waterhouse, London
August 1986

Foreword

Less than 15 years ago, in an era of relatively stable credit and currency markets, the treasurer's duties were straightforward. The operations he supervised were biased towards the efficient collection and disbursement of funds, investment of surplus funds in the interbank or short-term credit markets and the closing of the 'funds gap' by bank borrowing or the issuance of debentures. The introduction of floating exchange rates, heralded as the way of smoothing exchange fluctuations, has created volatile markets which are more influenced, on a short-term basis, by financial trading transactions than by commercial flows. Government emphasis on the control of economies by monetary policy has created equally volatile credit markets.

The treasurer's responsibility for reducing uncertainty by operating in the financial markets has become a great challenge. The business strategy of a corporation can only be implemented with a sound financial strategy, designed to reduce costs and risks. This may limit the number of opportunities which can be pursued by the business strategy.

To draw up such a strategy, the responsibilities of each business unit must be carefully defined. For example it is essential that accountabilities of operating units and the treasury function with respect to levels of foreign exchange exposure be specified. Controls and systems must be appropriate for the organisation; the methods of financing the corporation must be considered. The currency mix must be designed to achieve a known level of exposure; interest rate exposure patterns need to be determined; the duration of the financial liabilities needs to be compared with that of the assets of the enterprise. The level of debt and equity needs to be balanced, in part to create the earnings appropriate for each unit of equity and in part to reduce the after tax cost of capital.

Plans must allow for access to funds in the currencies, amounts and types needed. Exchange exposure must also be managed on a transactional basis. Relationships with banks and investors must be maintained.

Financial markets allow the treasurer flexibility to implement his plans. Reduction of barriers to capital flows has given him choices as to where to obtain funds. Securitisation of the credit markets has allowed an enterprise direct access to investors without a bank intermediary. It is not unusual to see a United Kingdom company with European business units borrowing short-term funds from the Deutschemark, yen, US dollar, or sterling markets. The availability of currency swaps can render these funds into other currencies, often more cheaply than borrowing directly in that form. Similarly, debt raised in floating-rate form can be fixed through the interest rate swap market.

The development of option markets has allowed the treasurer further to define, and reduce, business risks in the financial markets. Standard Oil's issuance of Oil-indexed Notes, designed to hedge the value of crude oil five years out, has allowed us to reduce the systematic price risk which affects our company's fortunes.

The treasurer needs to be wary of becoming lost in a sea of competing financial techniques and instruments and of regarding his role as management of these instruments. He is responsible for the overall strategic management of finance.

In performing his task the treasurer needs access to good information. The advent of modern treasury management systems and the availability of external information systems have helped him in his task. But above all his performance needs to be measured. Has he created value by hedging foreign exchange exposures? Has he made the right decisions in funding the corporation? By measuring the treasurer's performance he is made accountable for creating profit for a company. This does not create conflict with the financial system, provided that he conducts himself in a professional way. Subject to his finance strategy, he can create profit by trading for his own account in financial markets. The reduction of barriers between banker and treasurer has created new opportunities.

Much of the existing literature addresses specific technical instruments or tends to be somewhat general. This publication on treasury management, in two volumes, presents an integrated approach to managing treasury in successive levels of detail. The authors have presented the material within a sound framework for analysis.

This framework first addresses the techniques underlying the decisions that need to be taken by management. It then addresses the information and organisation needed to make those decisions.

I commend this publication to those responsible for formulating a corporation's approach to treasury management. It meets a need not easily fulfilled in management literature today. I am convinced that these volumes will assist in the development of modern treasury practice.

E J P Browne
Executive Vice President & Chief Financial Officer,
Standard Oil Company,
Cleveland, Ohio 44114

Introduction

This book reflects the organisation, systems and controls required by treasury management. These requirements have arisen through the emergence and growth of international treasury management. This growth is a function of the structural economic changes that have occurred within the last two decades:

(1) The radical transformation in the foreign exchange and money markets, leading to the development of more sophisticated instruments and

(2) The electronic systems to support treasury transactions.

The factors which have influenced the infrastructure to support treasury decision-making are highlighted below:

The need for sound treasury objectives

In response to the greater uncertainty in the currency, money and capital markets, international business has become more, rather than less, complex. With this greater level of complexity, both in the environment and in the instruments available from financial institutions to the corporate treasurer, there is a fundamental need for the treasury to have 'clear cut' and well thought through objectives. For example, should the treasury be a cost centre, or should it be a profit centre? If it is a profit centre; should it break even, should it earn moderate or should it earn extensive profits.

The losses incurred due to interest and foreign currency risk can often equate to the profit generated from an entire operating division. Companies normally spend a significant amount of time in developing standard costing systems and adequate cost controls. However, relative to these issues, the time and resources devoted to establishing the objectives and management approach to exposure for a treasury department are not significant.

The organisation of the treasury

The organisation of the treasury should be a direct function of the objectives of the treasury. The objectives must be agreed and sanctioned by the board of directors. They must be understood at the highest level. Interest and currency risk are threats and opportunities to the business and therefore no board of directors can escape from understanding the implications of these risks. The objectives of the treasury will define whether it is a cost or profit centre.

This decision will impact on the organisation. Will it be centralised or decentralised? If centralised, it will probably need more complex systems and a greater level of expertise than if decentralised. There is therefore a fundamental need for the organisation of the treasury to be developed to achieve the mission set for it and whether it is to be reactive or proactive in the international treasury environment.

More sophisticated instruments

The major changes in the foreign exchange and money markets have led to a demand for new instruments to enable companies to protect themselves from exposure to the risk of interest and exchange rate fluctuations. Currency and interest rate hedging techniques such as interest rate swaps, options, and future rate agreements have been developed and the market for these products is expanding.

Interest rate swaps were introduced in 1982 to take advantage of the differing access to money markets available to companies with different credit ratings. Interest rate swaps therefore enable an 'AAA' company to obtain fixed-rate debt. The bank stands as intermediary between the two parties and charges a fee for taking on the credit risk. The most recent introduction, the future rate agreement, was first used in 1984 and already the market for this product has an average value of contracts outstanding of $1 billion.

Banks are constantly developing products which attempt to limit interest or exchange rate risk and which they can sell to their corporate clients. Increasingly they are trying to move away from straight term lending as a source of income and into the development of other financial products which are fee and commission based.

Electronic treasury systems

Dealing in the volatile money and foreign exchange markets requires not only experienced dealers but an adequate back-up system as well. Both bank and company dealers are thus increasing their use of computerised systems as a means of monitoring and manipulating their positions.

For a corporate treasury many computerised systems are available, from packages to handle one particular feature of the treasury, such as a netting system, to complete 'treasury workstations', which are a management decision support tool for the whole corporate treasury. These systems are either supplied by banks or software houses or are produced by the companies themselves for their own use.

Banks also provide balance reporting systems which enable customers to obtain detailed on-line statement information on their accounts. These reporting systems are slowly becoming more popular but are resisted by many companies which can currently obtain the same information at no cost over the telephone. To combat this the banks are considering the idea of restricting their telephone services, thereby forcing the use of electronic reporting systems.

The increase in general office automation also means that treasury departments have access to computer systems which enable them to maintain their own databases. Companies now have the means to produce sophisticated forecast and historical information about their own activities which should result in more efficient management of treasury in the future.

Treasury management therefore strikes at the core of the business. For example, the UK exporter who has sterling costs of production and yet a Deutschemark price list has foreign currency exposure in the very nature of his business. A conversion from those sterling costs of production to the Deutschemark price list can affect that company's market share, turnover and ultimately its profitability.

Similarly, fluctuations in foreign exchange rates can often be so significant that an adverse movement can eliminate the operating profits generated by a whole division within a multinational group.

The manager of international finance, who in this book has been termed the treasurer, therefore needs a sound understanding not only of the currency, money and capital markets but also of how these affect the commercial nature of his business.

Structure

This book is divided into chapters which present the organisation, systems and controls required by the treasurer in executing treasury transactions. The first four chapters address the form of the treasury organisation both in its profit making and international dimensions.

Having established the organisation, the following chapters deal with the infrastructure of electronic banking and reporting systems, together with their associated networks, required for managing the international treasury function. Subsequent chapters then address the controls and performance measurement of the treasury and finally lead to a discussion of the principles for establishing worldwide banking relations.

Acknowledgements

We are grateful to the many individuals, corporations and financial institutions who have influenced the development of our thoughts over recent years. Particularly:

John Browne, Standard Oil
David Bury, Hawker Siddeley
Peter Collier, Metal Box
Geoffrey Comer, Hawker Siddeley
Julian Costley, Reuters
Stephen Crompton, Unigate
John Coles, Guinness
Matthew Devlin, Citibank
Simon Duffy, Guinness
Stephen East, Redland
Terry Fitt, Citibank
Jeremy Ford, Bankers Trust
Michael Garner, TI Group
John Giannotti, Bankers Trust
David Gibson, TSB, Channel Islands
Charles Goldfinger, SWIFT
Per Haugen, Norske Shell
John Heywood, Hambros Bank
Gareth Jones, Redland
Alfred Kenyon, City Business School
Jonathan Lester, West of England Ship Owners Insurance Services
Alec Nacamuli, SWIFT
Susan Ross, Reuters
Ian Rushby, BP Finance International
David Smith, Thorn EMI
Alan Stabler, TI Group
Graham Steward, Hambros Bank
David Westby, Metal Box
Mark Wood, Barclays Merchant Bank

The team approach that we have developed at Price Waterhouse is the result of the enthusiasm and commitment of many including Mark Austen and Paul Reyniers, (consultancy); Nigel Buchanan and Richard Kilsby (audit) and Mike Maskall (international tax and trade finance).

In addition, the contributions from key members of our specialised treasury group, notably Louann Hotson, Valerie Hawkes, Arun Aggarwal, Victor Abrams, Gwen Batchelor, Nick Hughes, Helen Lamell, Howard Lovell, Jane MacLennan, Ranil Perera, Ariel Salama and Chris Taylor has proved invaluable. Without the co-operation and goodwill of many this work would not have been possible.

Mark E Austen

Paul J Reyniers

Price Waterhouse, London
August 1986

CHAPTER 1

Organisational structure

The form of the treasury function will depend on the objectives that have been set by the board and financial management for its operation. Arising from that, it will depend on whether the treasury is to operate as a profit or cost centre, and hence whether it is to be centralised or decentralised.

In this chapter the role of treasury in the financial function is discussed under the assumption that a decision has been made in one case to decentralise and, in another case, to centralise the treasury. The organisational structures of the treasury function that are needed to manage the decisions and the information to underpin them are then described.

Treasury and the finance function

The treasury is an integral part of the finance function. If we go back 10 years or so the trend in most companies was to have a corporate finance function. Many of the treasury activities of today were managed by the corporate finance function with the help of the secretarial department. With the relaxation of fixed exchange rates in 1974 and foreign exchange controls in 1979 (in the United Kingdom) this group of people had to face new problems. Suddenly they had to face fluctuating exchange rates, rapidly rising inflation and they had to decide whether they were going to make a profit from currency trading or to protect themselves from potential losses.

A new breed of international finance executive developed which has now taken the form of treasury management. Appendix 1.1 describes the typical responsibilities of some key treasury personnel. It is interesting to note that with some companies there still is a separate corporate finance and treasury function.

To explore this division of duties in more detail take the following example. Assume that the return on investment required from the corporate plan is 15% compound growth per annum after tax over the next five years. With existing resources only 10% return on investment after tax can be achieved over the next five years. There is therefore a planning gap of 5% per annum. The corporate plan is developed to address a strategy to bridge this 5% gap.

This corporate plan may involve new product development, investments in a new factory and plant or, indeed, acquisition. The financial director is told that he will need to find $130 million per annum to fund this planning gap. The traditional corporate finance role would be to review the company's capital gearing and balance sheet structure and identify what method of financing should underpin this $130 million. Should it be equity or should it be debt?

If we assume that the financing decision is going to be debt then this is where the traditional treasury tasks take over. The treasury needs to identify the form of the debt, the banks that should be approached, the cost of the debt, the currency of the debt, the guarantees, warranties, cross default clauses and covenants that are required. It will have to manage the paperwork underpinning the financing and co-ordinate the legal requirements.

A decade or so ago the traditional role for handling this problem would be between corporate finance and the secretarial department. Now we find that the role is often handled in total by what is termed the treasury function. That is the corporate finance and treasury functions have merged.

Figure 1.1 sets out the place of the treasury development in the finance function. It lists the typical corporate finance and treasury tasks. However, in practice these are often undertaken by one department. It is normally an historical accident whether they are called treasury or corporate finance.

Figure 1.1: The finance function

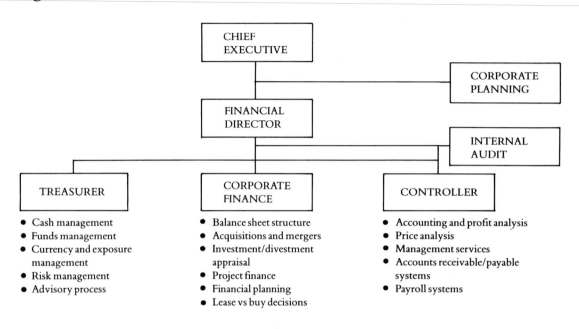

Capsule case

An interesting case of how the treasury and corporate finance functions separated rather than merged is that of a multinational manufacturer of consumable household products. Here the corporate finance function is based in the United Kingdom and the treasury in Europe. The corporate finance function manages policy formulation for group gearing, financing operations and acquisitions. It manages all tasks related to short, medium and long-term financing as well as banking, stock exchange and investor relations.

The treasury function on the other hand manages cashflow forecasting and all tasks related to placing surplus short-term investments, currency clearing and managing exposure. The treasury also manages banking (relations relevant to foreign exchange) and regulatory controls. This dual operation of corporate finance and treasury is an excellent example of a division of duties along the traditional lines.

The decentralised treasury function

If it is assumed that the treasury will operate on a decentralised basis then it is likely that there will be a small head office treasury team. Each individual operating group would then be left to manage its own treasury affairs. The activities of each decentralised treasury would vary country to country between the various operating groups. The key role of the small head office treasury would then be to ensure that policies and guidelines are issued so that they are able to manage their affairs but within the overall guidelines set by the group.

The small head office team may need to provide resources of an ad-hoc basis to operating groups should specific problems arise.

The advantages and disadvantages of a decentralised treasury function are set out in Table 1.1.

Table 1.1 - The advantages and disadvantages of a decentralised treasury

Advantages	*Disadvantages*
Autonomy for local treasury functions	Opportunity costs of the benefits associated with centralisation, such as netting or central banking
Suitable method of operation for many smaller companies	More treasury personnel are required in regional offices. This can result in higher overall staff costs
Only a small head office treasury department is required	

Capsule case

A number of multinational organisations operate on a decentralised treasury structure. In one particular case in point, the treasury policy is to have decentralised treasury action taken by operating groups. The operating groups are therefore responsible for relating their own policies, their own hedging programme, their own recruitment of treasury staff and their management of currency exposure.

All these treasury activities, including placing investments and raising short-term finance, are undertaken with a framework of broad policy guidelines. Such guidelines are set by a small head office team and include, for example:

● The group will not speculate in foreign currencies where speculation means buying or selling in foreign currency with no underlying commercial transaction
● The group will aim to match like currency receipts with payment including financing
● Group operated companies will net out intercompany transactions through a centrally run netting system
● All long-term financing must be approved by the centre
● All operating groups will submit returns as required by the centre.

Periodically the centre sends out technical papers to the operating groups on matters of treasury management, for example, on currency options and reinforces the general policies on exposure. The manner in which each operating group manages its exposure results in gains or losses which ultimately feed through into the accounts and are included in the figures for which those subsidiaries are judged on performance.

The centralised treasury function

If we can assume now that an alternative decision has been taken by the board that the treasury should be centralised then the way in which this centralisation is structured can take a number of forms. These forms are total centralisation, regionalisation and centralisation based on pooling of cash.

In total centralisation, all treasury tasks are incorporated at the centre and no subsidiary unit can place investments, raise finance, or handle any currency transactions through a bank over a certain minimum level. That minimum level will be required for normal operating purposes, for example, purchase of travellers cheques and small operating cashflows.

In the case of regionalisation, the central treasury function has split up the management of treasury on a worldwide scale. These regions for treasury may correspond to regional business areas or alternatively, may correspond to capital centres such as London, New York and Tokyo. The UK multinational groups tend to have regional treasury functions based in, for example, London or Brussels for the European region and which manage the treasury activities of that region.

Table 1.2 - The advantages and disadvantages of centralised treasury

Advantages	*Disadvantages*
Cost and exposure savings can be achieved through netting and other techniques	Local treasury functions loss autonomy
Fewer treasury personnel are required in regional offices; expertise is concentrated at the centre	A larger head office treasury function is required

Capsule case

A well known US based manufacturing company has set up a centralised treasury in London to manage its European activities. Typically, the tasks of this function include the pooling of all investment and finance transactions.

In addition, the treasury function issues internal forward contracts for subsidiaries, thereby taking on the exposure at the centre. The central treasury is run by a small team of highly experienced (and expensive) professionals. For tax purposes it is set up as a separate finance company.

Thirdly, where a treasury centre is based in a capital market for the sole purpose of pooling cash where there are also tax benefits, then the treasury can be centralised by cash pool, for example in Luxembourg, Bermuda or Brussels. A number of the commodity companies have adopted treasury organisations centred by cash pool as they are in a position based on the numerous transactions to divert cash resources to these capital markets.

The location of the treasury function, if centralised, could be at the head office due to historical accident, as a power base for management structure or for communication to other departments. Alternatively, the location of the centralised treasury might be based in a tax haven.

The treasury organisation structure

The treasury organisational structure for a centralised treasury needs to include professionals to handle the key areas of treasury information decision-making. An example of such a treasury function has been structured for a major company and is set out in Figure 1.2.

Key action points

The key action points that arise from this chapter are as follows:

- (1) Define clear policies for the treasury function agreed by the board.
- (2) Based on (1) assess whether the treasury should be a cost or profit centre.
- (3) Based on (2) assess whether the treasury should be centralised or decentralised.
- (4) Choose location of the treasury based on centralisation requirements and appropriate tax regime.

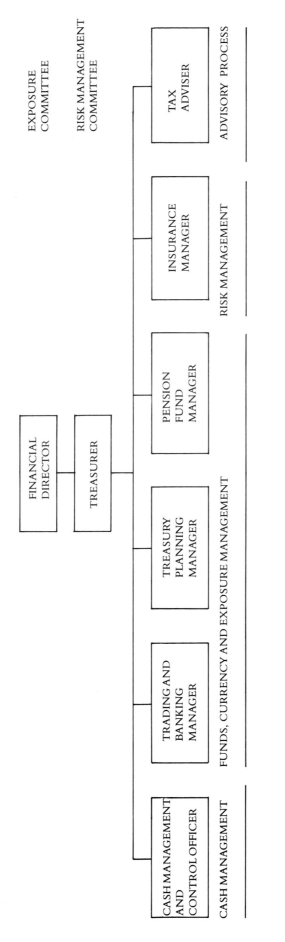

Figure 1.2: The treasury function

The treasury function

Summary job description: treasurer responsible to: financial director

Main tasks

Objectives/policies/procedures

1   Set and review objectives and policies for the treasury department.

2   Review and ensure conformity to procedures set out in the Treasury Policies and Procedures Manual.

3   Set and review the responsibilities of all members of the treasury department.

4   Set and review the evaluation procedures for all members of the treasury department.

5   Ensure briefing of members of the treasury department.

6   Propose and review a succession plan for members of the treasury department.

Advisory process

7   Active member of a foreign exchange exposure group.

8   Active member of a risk management group.

9   Set and review work programmes for each element of the advisory process.

10   Actively encourage consultation and advice on treasury matters to other sections and departments of the organisation.

Management of treasury

11   Day to day decisions involving all information and decision areas.

Summary job description: cash management & control officer responsible to: treasurer

Main tasks

Objectives/policies/procedures

1   Review and agree objectives and policies with the treasurer on:

—Working capital management

—Cash collection and disbursement

—Netting and pooling of funds.

Analysis

2   Identify, review and evaluate the existing methods of collecting and disbursing cash.

3   Liaise and advise accounts receivable/payable on the efficiency of receiving/paying cash.

4   Identify and evaluate the costs and benefits of operating the netting and pooling systems.

Transaction accounting

5   Administer and record:

—Domestic and foreign currency transactions

—Letters of credit, acceptances, and guarantees

—Investment, funding and hedging transactions.

Forecasting and reporting

6   Prepare short-term (daily/monthly) forecasts as required by the treasury planning manager and set out in the Treasury Policies and Procedures Manual.

7   Maintain the treasury reporting system as specified by the treasury planning manager and set out in the Treasury Policies and Procedures Manual.

Summary job description: trading and banking manager
responsible to: treasurer

Main tasks

Objectives/policies/procedures

1   Set, review and agree objectives, policies and procedures with the treasurer on:

    —Banking relations and control

    —Short-term investments and funding

    —Foreign exchange transactions

    —Monitoring, forecasting and reporting external information.

Banking relations and control

2   Identify information requirements.

3   Control opening and closing of bank accounts.

4   Review counterparty limits.

5   Manage and review banking relations.

Trading

6   Identify, execute and evaluate transactions relating to:

    —Local and foreign currencies

    —Short-term investments and funding

    —Hedging exposure.

Forecasting and reporting

7   Prepare and distribute forecasts of external information.

8   Review the accuracy of forecasts and report on 6 above.

Summary job description: treasury planning manager
responsible to: treasurer

Main tasks

Objectives/policies/procedures

1   Set, review and agree objectives, policies and procedures with the treasurer on:

    —Controlling, forecasting and reporting internal information

    —Long-term investment and funding

    —Hedging exposure.

Financial management

2   Identify and evaluate long-term investment options.

3   Co-ordinate and advise evaluation teams in the case of acquisitions.

4   Identify and evaluate long-term funding options.

5   Co-ordinate bankers and lawyers re 2 to 4 above.

6   Identify and collate loan agreements, covenants and warranties.

Exposure management

7   Identify and assess exposure.

8   Define a hedging strategy for exposure.

Forecasting and reporting

9   Design and maintain a framework for identifying information required by treasury.

10 Manage the treasury forecasting system.

11 Manage the treasury reporting system.

12 Supervise completion of the treasury reporting package defined in the Policies and Procedures Manual.

Miscellaneous

13 Advise and assist the treasurer in the advisory process.

14 Prepare the reporting package for the exposure committee.

15 Assist the treasurer in risk management matters.

16 Assess and co-ordinate automation requirements of the treasury department.

CHAPTER 2

The treasury operational framework

The previous chapter considered the alternative structures of a treasury function. This chapter aims to provide a structure for deriving treasury objectives and policies and to illustrate by way of example how such policies could appear in a treasury operations manual.

It is disconcerting that little emphasis is often placed on ensuring that the treasury department has formalised, agreed and documented objectives and policies. Corporate treasurers who consider themselves to conduct treasury activities in a risk adverse manner will often expose themselves to risk by the absence of such documented guidelines for activity.

Treasury activity is not only fairly technical and complex to the non-treasurer, but it is also distinct from the business activity of the company and therefore the terms of reference for treasury operations should be agreed and clearly understood by both senior management and those in the treasury function. Otherwise there is a risk that the senior management will have false expectations for the treasury, and explanations such as 'the US dollar was forecast to weaken' may fall on unsympathetic ears.

Determining treasury objectives and policies

The first step in setting up the treasury operational framework is to determine the objectives and policies of the treasury function. This step is crucial and affects the direction of treasury activities. It is necessary first to determine the overall objective of the treasury function, and from this to develop detailed policies and guidelines for the management of the treasury function.

However, in determining these objectives and policies, management do not have a 'green field' open to them, but rather must operate within certain parameters, as illustrated in Figure 2.1.

This figure shows three categories of constraints on the treasury objectives, policies and activities which are discussed further below.

External factors over which the company has no control

These are influences on the company's business which arise from the marketplace in which the company trades. Examples are competitive pressures from other companies; the types of customers with whom the company trades (for example, a high volume of low sales values or few customers of high sales value); the lead time between orders received and goods provided; and the sensitivity of the company's profitability to interest and exchange rate movements.

The key external factors which influence treasury decisions are those factors which have an impact on the currencies, amounts and, most importantly, the predictability of a company's cashflows. This is because the cashflow forecast, as discussed in Volume I, is a vital source of information to the treasurer, upon which he bases his decisions and activities.

Assessing the degree of certainty with which cashflows are predicted is an activity to which many treasurers devote significant attention because the conclusions directly impact their hedging strategy.

Figure 2.1: Parameters in setting treasury objectives and policies

EXTERNAL FACTORS OVER WHICH THE COMPANY HAS NO CONTROL

- Characteristics of the marketplace in which the company is trading:
  — Competitive pressures
  — Customer profiles
  — Currencies, amounts and predictability of cashflows
  — Velocity of sales and production cycles
- Banking and advisory services available
- Exchange rate volatility
- Interest rate volatility.

INTERNAL TO THE TREASURY DEPARTMENT

- Group Treasury structure:
  — Geographic and functional spread of treasury centres, staff and other resources
  — Centralisation vs decentralisation
- Organisational structure and numbers, quality and areas of competence of staff (eg banking, accountancy, computerisation, taxation, legalities)
- Other resources available.

INTERNAL TO THE COMPANY BUT OUTSIDE THE TREASURY FUNCTION

- Senior management objectives and expectations of the treasury function
- Company/group organisational structure, tiers of management, and their understanding of treasury management
- Company business objectives and strategies
- Geographical structure of the company/group.

Let us consider for a moment how the competitive pressures from other companies can affect treasury decisions. By way of example, let us assume that there are two identical companies both in the timber business. Both companies are intending to buy timber from the same supplier abroad in May and to sell the timber on to firms of builders. It is January when the timber is ordered and when the price is fixed in the foreign currency. Therefore both companies now have an exposure to foreign exchange rate fluctuations for the timber ordered.

However, it is not simply a question of the best means of hedging the exposure because there are competitive pressures to evaluate as well. For example, say that company A decides to cover the exposure by means of a forward foreign exchange contract, an action which is normally considered to be prudent, and company B leaves the exposure uncovered. Should the exchange rate then move favourably before payment is due such that the cost of the goods declines, then company B will have a reduced price to pay for its goods. However, company A is locked into a price determined by the forward foreign exchange contract, therefore company B could be in a position to undercut the sale price of company A even though the treasurer of company A was 'prudent'. This example shows the influence which competitive pressures may have on treasury decisions.

Factors which are internal to the company but outside the treasury function

These are factors which are within the control of the senior management of a company but are outside the corporate treasurer's jurisdiction. It is at this level that the overall objective for having a treasury function is set and the expectations of the department are determined. It is at this level that senior management will face such key issues as whether the treasury function should be a cost centre or profit centre.

In defining the boundaries of the corporate treasurer's responsibilities and scope for action, the organisational structure and degree of treasury competence at senior management level are important.

The corporate treasurer who reports directly to the board of directors, none of whom have more than a passing knowledge of treasury matters, will usually carry more responsibility and have a wider scope for action than the corporate treasurer who reports to the finance director, who used to fill the corporate treasurer's position, and who has several tiers of management above his position.

To give an indication of the overall treasury objectives adopted by companies in Europe, Figure 2.2 is included. This presents the results of a market research project by Business International Corporation, and is interesting because it shows that the top two objectives are to minimise borrowing needs and costs and to minimise currency risks and transaction costs, whereas to maximise returns on cash investment ranks much lower in importance.

Figure 2.2: Top cash management objectives in Europe (ranked by 302 companies on a weighted average basis*)

(1)	Minimise borowing needs and costs	44.6
(2)	Minimise currency risks and transaction costs	41.7
(3)	Minimise idle bank balances	27.3
(4)	Minimise customer delays and bad debt	26.2
(5)	Maximise returns on cash investments	11.7
(6)	Minimise funds transfer costs	10.3
(7)	Minimise overall tax liabilities	8.5
(8)	Maximise remittances from subsidiaries	7.3
(9)	Maximise terms/delays to suppliers	3.0

* Under the weighted average computation, objectives ranked most important were given a weight of 100 points; those ranked second were given a weight of 60 points; and those ranked third were given a weight of 20 points. The points were added and then divided by the total number of respondents. Hence, weighted average ranking for each objective will range from 0 to 100; the higher the number, the greater the importance of the objective.

SOURCE: Business International Corporation

Factors which are internal to the treasury department

The final and closest set of constraints on the activities of the treasury department are the geographical and operational structure of the department and the resources available. The objectives and expectations of the treasury function must be attainable with the resources available. This refers both to physical resources such as microcomputers and to staff resources. The numbers of employees and their particular areas of competence (for example, banking, accountancy, computerisation, taxation, legalities) are relevant.

Structure of the treasury operations manual

This section aims to illustrate by way of example how the treasury objectives and policies would appear in a treasury operations manual. It is most important that a treasury operations manual is prepared once the overall objective of the treasury function has been carefully agreed and noted. There are four key sections to a treasury operations manual:

● Delegation of authority
● Treasury objectives and administrative policies
● Authority limits
● Exception reporting criteria.

Each of these groups is discussed in outline below and supported by a detailed appendix.

Delegation of authority

The delegation of authority from the chief executive to the chief financial officer, and from the chief financial officer to the treasurer must be specified and agreed for each main treasury transaction or group of transactions. A pro-forma checklist of the areas for clarification is included as Appendix 2.1

Treasury objectives and administrative policies

Once the scope of the treasury's activities has been defined it is necessary to formulate 'sub-objectives' for each area of the treasury function and to formulate administrative policies. These policies are the base rules by which the treasury should operate in order to achieve its objectives. Illustrative examples of treasury objectives and administrative policies are set out in Appendix 2.2 for:

- Internal information requirements
- External information requirements
- Cash management
- Funds management
- Currency and exposure management.

Authority limits

Within the administrative policies, authority limits should be set which regulate the action that may be taken by dealing staff. These authority limits specify the currency, amount, type and timing of investments, financing and currency dealing and hedging transactions which each member of the treasury is authorised to transact.

The objective of having authority limits is that dealing staff have defined boundaries within which they are authorised to operate. This provides the treasury with a measure of control. Examples of authority limits are set out in Appendix 2.3.

Exception reporting criteria

The final element of control on treasury activities is represented by exception reporting criteria. These are pre-defined measures of treasury activity which if exceeded must be communicated to management immediately.

Exception criteria should therefore relate either to a breach of authority or to a measure of activity which has important ramifications for treasury decision-making. A summary of exception criteria is set out in Appendix 2.4 for illustrative purposes.

Key action points

The following are the key treasury action points arising in this chapter:

- Every corporate treasury function should have formalised, agreed and documented objectives and policies contained in the treasury operations manual.
- The first step in determining the treasury operational framework is to determine the objectives and policies of the treasury function. These must be set within the constraints of external factors governing the operation of the company, such as the marketplace and services available and internal constraints such as resources available and senior management objectives.
- The treasury operations manual should detail objectives and policies for the delegation of authority, administrative policies, authority limits and exception reporting criteria.

APPENDIX 2.1

Example of delegation of authority by chief executive and chief financial officer

Action	CE's Delegation to CFO *	CFO's Delegation to Treasury *
CASH INVESTMENT		
1 Opening deposit and investment accounts in all currencies.		
2 Placing short-term local currency investments in banks. No investment will be made where the amount exceeds 40% of the equity of the recipient institution.		
3 Placing short-term local currency investments in insurance companies.		
4 Placing short-term foreign currency investments in banks. will be made where the amount exceeds 40% of the equity of the recipient institution. used their limits should be defined by central treasury. No investment will be made where the amount exceeds 40% of the equity of the recipient. Where foreign banks are used their limits should be defined by central treasury.		
5 Placing long-term local currency investments.		
6 Placing long-term foreign currency investments.		
FINANCING REQUIREMENTS		
7 Opening short-term funding accounts in local and foreign currencies.		
8 Drawing on short-term local currency facilities.		
9 Drawing on short-term foreign currency facilities.		
10 Increasing short-term local or foreign currency facilities.		
11 Raising short-term finance (less than two years).		
12 Raising long-term finance.		
CURRENCY AND EXPOSURE MANAGEMENT		
13 Spot currency purchase and sales for specific operating transactions.		
14 Undertaking hedging transactions.		

*   Entries made in these columns should be based on financial policies and be agreed by the policy committee of the company.

APPENDIX 2.2

Objectives and administrative policies

System: internal information requirements

Objective	*Administrative Policy*
To provide the treasury department, management and head office with accurate, consistent and timely reports on:	The treasury department routines for reporting internal information are as follows:

1 Cash management	1 Maintenance and annual review of treasury department objectives, policies and procedures for reporting internal information.
2 Funds management	2 Production of rolling cashflows by currency.
3 Currency and exposure management.	3 Production and distribution of reports according to an agreed timetable and distribution schedule.
	4 Production of reports which match the format, detail, and frequency requirements of treasury, and management.

System: external information requirements

Objective	*Administrative Policy*
To identify and monitor the external information required by the treasury department. To forecast and report this external information so as to provide a tool for treasury decision-making.	The treasury department routines for monitoring, forecasting and reporting external information should include the following:

	1 Maintenance and annual review of treasury department objectives, policies and procedures for external information.
	2 Identifying, collecting and cataloguing external information.
	3 Annual review of the external information requirements of the treasury department.
	4 Continual evaluation of the validity of external information (including external services from banks and agencies) so as to form a treasury view.
	5 Communication of significant trends in external information to financial management.

System: cash management; sub-system: cash collections

Objective

To analyse, evaluate and comment on the most efficient methods and procedures for collecting cash. The over-riding objective is to minimise the time it takes to invoice a customer and receive good value for funds. This is termed 'float' time.

Administrative Policy

The treasury department routines for cash collections should include the following:

1 Maintenance and annual review of treasury department objectives, policies and procedures for analysing, evaluating and commenting on the efficiency of cash collection methods.

2 Identification, review and evaluation of existing and alternative methods of collecting cash in terms of:

   a Internal processing costs

   b Float delays caused by customer, internal processing and bank routing

   c Obtaining discounts.

3 Liaison with, and advice to, management of accounts receivable on cash collection monitoring systems.

System: cash management; sub-system: cash disbursements

Objective

To analyse, evaluate and comment on the most efficient methods and procedures for disbursing cash. The over-riding objective is to maximise the time between being invoiced and losing good value on funds. This is termed 'reverse float' time.

Administrative Policy

The treasury department routines for cash disbursements should include the following:

1 Maintenance and annual review of treasury department objectives, policies and procedures for analysing, evaluating and commenting on the efficiency of cash disbursement methods.

2 Identification, review and evaluation of existing and alternative methods of disbursing cash in terms of:

   a Internal processing costs

   b Reverse float methods

   c Payment discounts and overdue interest payments.

3 Liaison with, and advice to, management of accounts payable on cash disbursement monitoring systems (for instance categorising follow-up practices and procedures of suppliers).

4 Achievement of 2 and 3 without jeopardising relationships with suppliers.

System: cash management; sub-system: intercompany transfers (netting) and cash centralisation (pooling)

Objective

To use group netting and pooling facilities, where they are financially advantageous, according to the policies set by the central treasury.

Administrative Policy

The treasury department routines for netting and pooling should include the following:

1   Maintenance and annual review of treasury department objectives, policies and procedures for using netting and pooling facilities.

2   Ensuring that treasury are familiar with the latest netting and pooling facilities on offer from banks.

3   Utilisation of the netting and pooling facilities in 2 where these are financially advantageous.

4   Periodic evaluation of the costs and benefits of using the netting and pooling facilities on offer.

System: funds management; sub-system: short-term investments

Objective

To maximise the return on investment given an acceptable level of risk.

Administrative Policy

The treasury department routines for making short-term investments should include the following:

1   Maintenance and annual review of treasury department objectives, policies and procedures for investing cash.

2   Achievement of the investment objective by:

    a   Fully utilising cash resources available for short-term investments

    b   Obtaining the best available market rate.

3   Undertaking 2 in accordance with authority limits set out in the treasury operations manual and revised from time to time.

4   Possible restriction of short-term investments to certain financial institutions such as banks and finance companies.

5   Possible restriction on the level of investment such as:

    a   No local short-term investment to exceed 40% of the equity of recipient institutions.

    b   No foreign short-term investment to exceed amounts agreed by head office.

6   The investment decision should be based on the following criteria in addition to type of investment.

    a   Security

    b   Liquidity

    c   Yield

7   Execution of transactions in accordance with group policies.

NOTE: As a result of investment policies (2 to 7 above) it may be necessary to move investments from one institution to the other. The overall policy is that the investments should:

(1)   Be placed to provide the best return
(2)   Be distributed between banks as evenly as possible where net returns are identical.

System: funds management; sub-system: long-term financing

Objective	Administrative Policy
The objective of raising long-term funds (over two years) is to finance long-term cashflow requirements in a manner consistent with the financial strategy and structure of the group.	The treasury department routines for raising long-term finance should include the following: 1 Maintenance and annual review of treasury department objectives, policies and procedures for raising long-term finance. 2 Co-ordination of long-term financing decisions. 3 Prohibition of long-term financing decisions without prior discussions with top level management and financial advisors.

System: funds management; sub-system: short-term financing

Objective

The objective of raising short-term funds (less than two years) is to finance short-term cashflow requirements.

Administrative Policy

The treasury department routines for raising short-term finance should include the following:

1   Maintenance and annual review of treasury department objectives, policies and procedures for raising short-term finance.

2   The funding objective should be achieved by:

   a   Identifying the amount to be funded

   b   Obtaining these funds at the lowest relative cost.

3   Undertaking 2 in accordance with authority limits set out in the treasury operations manual and revised from time to time.

4   Annual review of credit facilities and terms provided by banks.

5   Possible restrictions on short-term finance such as:

   a   Financing through local institutions to be agreed by the chief financial officer

   b   Financing through foreign institutions to be referred to head office management.

6   Ensuring that overdraft facilities are not exceeded.

7   Ensuring that short-term finance is not obtained by postponing payments to local suppliers or tax authorities

8   Basing the financial decision on the following criteria:

   a   Cost of funds

   b   Guarantees required

   c   Flexibility

   d   Other bank conditions and warranties.

9   Raising finance in accordance with group policies issued from time to time.

System: currency and exposure management; sub-system: dealing foreign exchange exposure

Objective	*Administrative Policy*
To minimise exposure to foreign exchange risk by adopting hedging techniques.	The treasury department routines for managing foreign exchange and exposure should include the following:

1 Maintenance and annual review of treasury department objectives, policies and procedures for currency and exposure management.

2 Execution of spot forward and swap transaction according to counterparty and authority limits.

3 Preparation of a hedging plan to protect the company from exposed (unmatched) transactions.

4 Identification of matched and unmatched transactions.

5 Evaluation of alternative internal and external hedging techniques for particular transactions.

6 Undertaking hedging transactions according to authority limits and exception reporting criteria.

7 Review of the applicability of internal and external hedging techniques from time to time.

8 Undertaking of hedging programmes which are in accordance with group policies.

APPENDIX 2.3

Authority limits

System: funds management; sub-system: short-term investments

	Event	Personnel Authorised *	Authority Limit
1	Placing local currency investments	Treasurer	Amount .... Timing ....
2	Placing $ investments	Treasurer	Amount .... Timing ....
3	Placing DM investments	Treasurer	Amount .... Timing ....
4	Placing other foreign currency investments	Treasurer	Amount .... Timing ....
5	Use of pooling facilities	Treasurer	Amount .... Timing ....

Note:

For purposes of applying authority limits, investments are defined as amounts placed in accounts on a short-term basis to obtain the best returns and liquidity position.

*Job titles listed in this column are used for illustrative purposes only.

System: funds management; sub-system: financing

	Event	Personnel Authorised *	Authority Limit
1	Raising long-term finance	Finance Director	All long-term funding in local or foreign currencies greater than .... should be sanctioned by top management (the board)
2	Raising short-term finance in local currency on existing facilities	Finance Director	Amount .... Timing ....
3	Raising short-term finance in foreign currency on existing facilities	Finance Director	Amount .... Timing ....
4	Opening new short-term funding accounts in local or foreign currencies	Finance Director	Amount .... Timing ....
5	Utilisation of short-term finance facilities in local currency	Treasurer	(1) Amount .... Timing .... (2) Amount .... Timing ....
6	Utilisation of short-term finance facilities in foreign currencies	Treasurer	(1) Amount .... Timing .... (2) Amount .... Timing ....

System: currency and exposure management; sub-system: currency management

	Event	Personnel Authorised *	Limit/Action
1	Spot purchase and sale transactions relating to receivables/payables in the ordinary course of business	Treasurer	By currency Amount .... Timing .... Counterparty ....
2	Spot purchase and sale transactions outside the ordinary course of business (for example, as part of a hedge)	Treasurer	By currency Amount .... Timing .... Counterparty ....

System: currency and exposure management; sub-system: exposure management

Event	Personnel Authorised *	Limit/Action
Hedging foreign exchange exposure including: (1) Technique to be adopted (2) Amount of hedge (3) Timing of hedge.	All action to be agreed by (1) Treasurer (2) Financial Director.	By currency: Amount .... Timing .... Counterparty ....

APPENDIX 2.4

Exception reporting criteria

System	Event	Personnel Involved *	Action Required *
1 INVESTING CASH	1.1 Breach of authority limits	All treasury personnel	Cash management and control officer prepares exception report to the treasurer and financial director
	1.2 More than £/$/DM etc .... million is held in short term investments	Trading and banking manager	
	1.3 More than £ .... million equivalent is held in other currencies (to 1.2 above)	Trading and banking manager	
2 FUNDING CASH REQUIREMENTS	2.1 Breach of authority limits	All treasury personnel	Cash management and control officer prepares exception report to the treasurer and financial director
	2.2 Utilisation of overdraft facilities exceeds ....%	Trading and banking manager	
3 FOREIGN EXCHANGE TRANSACTIONS	3.1 Breach of authority limits	All treasury personnel	Cash management and control officer prepares exception report to the treasurer and financial director
	3.2 Weekly foreign exchange spot purchases exceed £/$/DM etc .... million	Trading and banking manager	
	3.3 Weekly foreign exchange spot sales exceed £/$/DM etc .... million	Trading and banking manager	
4 EXPOSURE MANAGEMENT	4.1 Breach of authority limits	All treasury personnel	Cash management and control officer prepares exception report to the treasurer and financial director
	4.2 Cumulative value of forward purchase contracts exceeds £/$/DM etc .... million	Trading and banking manager	
	4.3 Cumulative value of forward sales contracts exceeds £/$/DM etc .... million	Trading and banking manager	
	4.4 Notional gain/loss on open forward contracts exceeds £ .... million	Trading and banking manager	
	4.5 Actual gain/loss on closed forward contracts exceeds £ .... million	Trading and banking manager	

*Job titles listed in these columns are for illustrative purposes.

CHAPTER 3

The role of the group treasury function

The role adopted by a group treasury function is a major factor influencing its treasury management reporting requirements. For example, the group treasury which acts purely as advisor to subsidiary companies, where all treasury decisions are made, will require a reporting system which merely collects and collates information at the group level, with individual modelling, recording and reporting systems at subsidiary level. On the other hand, for treasuries where the group treasury acts as banker to the subsidiaries and where all treasury decision-making is centralised at group level, a sophisticated modelling, recording and reporting system will be required by group treasury and basic information transmitting facilities will be required at subsidiary level.

This chapter builds upon the structural and operational factors already considered in this volume. It first discusses the role of the group treasury function, and in particular considers the growing trend for corporate treasuries to bypass the banking sector by providing their own 'in-house' services. The impact of the role of the group treasury function on the treasury reporting requirements is then considered.

The role of the group treasury function is a separate, but related issue to the question of centralisation vs decentralisation. Whereas the latter concerns the level in the group structure at which the treasury decision-making should be performed (for example, at subsidiary or group level); the role of the treasury function discussed in this chapter concerns the way in which the group's banking relationships are managed, and the extent to which external commercial and merchant banking services are required.

For discussion purposes, three classifications are identified in this chapter of the role of the group treasury function. These classifications are not discrete categories with firm boundaries and a particular treasury function may straddle more than one role. These are:

- An advisory role, whereby the group treasury function is simply an information source to subsidiaries, branches or divisions; providing information on market rates and prices and advice on possible courses of treasury action. Treasury management decision-making is undertaken at the subsidiary, branch or division level, and this role is associated with a decentralised treasury management structure
- An agency role, whereby the group treasury function conducts the group's treasury transactions and negotiations on behalf of the individual subsidiaries, branches or divisions. Treasury management decision-making may be undertaken at either group or subsidiary etc level; thereby enabling this approach to be used in both centralised and decentralised treasury structures
- A banking role, whereby the group treasury performs intragroup clearing and matching of treasury requirements and only uses an external bank's services for those requirements which cannot be met by the corporate treasury. This role implies at least partial centralisation of the treasury function.

Many group corporate treasury departments today began in an advisory role and evolved into an agency role as the company grew and as exchange rates and interest rates became more volatile in the 1970s resulting in the need for a co-ordinated group treasury management approach. In very recent years some of the corporate treasuries of the larger companies with good credit-ratings, fairly low gearing and in-house banking expertise have moved more forcefully into a banking role.

The threat of 'disintermediation' is now beginning to concern the banking sector. Disintermediation is the term used to describe the process of corporations conducting traditional banking activities such as finance and investment between themselves without the use of a bank. For example, large 'AAA' credit-rated companies are beginning to issue their own Eurobonds without the use of a bank. Often in these cases a company's own 'AAA' credit rating is higher than that of many banks who have recently suffered loan losses, for instance, to Latin American countries. Therefore, the companies often feel that it is preferable to issue bonds in their own names rather than through a lesser-rated bank.

The remainder of this chapter will consider the advisory, agency and banking roles each in turn. We will then dwell on how to evaluate the relative costs and benefits of the various roles. The impact on a treasury's reporting system is then followed by a summary of the key points raised in this chapter.

Advisory role

In this capacity, a group treasury's prime function is to provide an in-house information source to the treasury centres of the group. This role assumes a decentralised treasury management structure, with all decision-making being performed at treasury centre level.

In meeting its aims, the group treasury will need to perform several tasks:

- The group treasury should provide a central database (whether by computerised or manual means) of relevant market information. This includes indications of current and forecast market interest and exchange rates and securities prices for a suitable range of instruments
- The group treasury should analyse and interpret market information in order to aid treasury centres in determining the appropriate course of treasury action
- A key task of the group treasury is to provide treasury expertise by understanding the mechanics and applications of the complete range of instruments, products and services available to the corporate treasury.

Figure 3.1: Example: Advisory role of the group treasury function

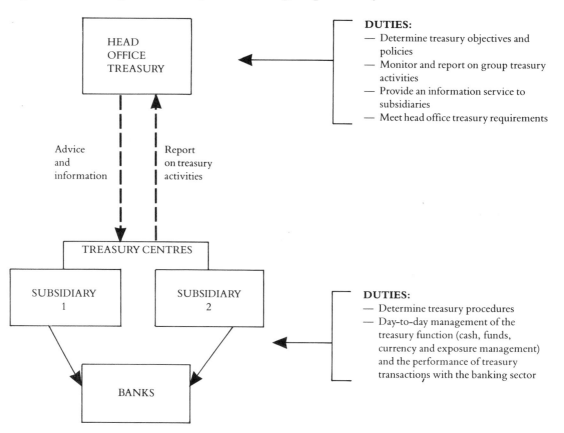

Figure 3.1 provides a possible treasury structure in which the head office treasury adopts an advisory role. It will be noted that the head office treasury provides the treasury centres, in this case two subsidiaries, with advice and information only and that decisions are made by the subsidiaries. Contact with the banks is performed by the individual subsidiaries. Head office prepares consolidated reports of treasury activities from the returns submitted by subsidiaries.

The major benefit of a centralised advisory function in a decentralised treasury is that a higher degree of expertise can be justified on cost/benefit grounds to service a number of treasury centres than to service individual treasury centres. Also, duplication of information gathering and analysis tasks is avoided.

Agency role

In adopting an agency role, the group treasury maintains the banking relationships on behalf of the group and performs banking and treasury transactions on instruction from and on behalf of the treasury centres. Additionally the group treasury will often fulfil an advisory role. The performance of these two roles is illustrated in Figure 3.2. In this example, the treasury decision-making is decentralised, but this structure could function equally as well with a centralised approach to decision-making.

Figure 3.2 shows the flows of advice and information from the head office treasury to the individual subsidiaries, who then determine the treasury action to be taken and instruct the head office treasury to conduct this action on the subsidiaries' behalf with the bankers to the group.

Figure 3.2: Example: Agency role of the group treasury function

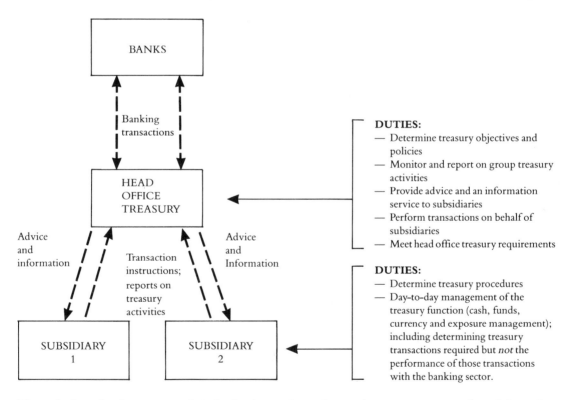

The major benefit of an agency role is that banking relationships and transactions are conducted through a central department therefore enabling a centralised dealing function to make most efficient use of the group's resources. The necessity to have dealing expertise within each of the treasury centres is avoided, and volumes of transactions are concentrated on a limited number of banks with whom the group becomes a more valued customer than if the banking relationships are dispersed across the group and a greater number of banks.

An agency role is suitable where a prime objective of the group is to have complete autonomy and accountability for each operating unit (subsidiary, branch, division or other means of segregating activities). However the major loss with an agency role compared to a banking role is the total group-wide view of treasury activities and the netting of the requirements of the group's operating units prior to approaching the group's bankers.

Banking role

The banking role has been the most recent to evolve and is continuing to evolve as technology develops which enables the corporate treasurer to control and manage his treasury activities more closely. Corporate treasurers in recent years have become more aggressive and sparing in their transactions with banks, placing greater emphasis on obtaining competitive quotations and lower bank charges, and performing intercompany clearing of transactions and matching of requirements where possible.

Figure 3.3 illustrates a treasury structure where a banking role is adopted by the head office treasury. In the illustration shown, the treasury decision-making is partially decentralised, with responsibility for identifying and hedging exposure resting with the subsidiaries; however, the subsidiaries are obliged to deal with the head office treasury.

Figure 3.3: Example: Banking role of the group treasury function

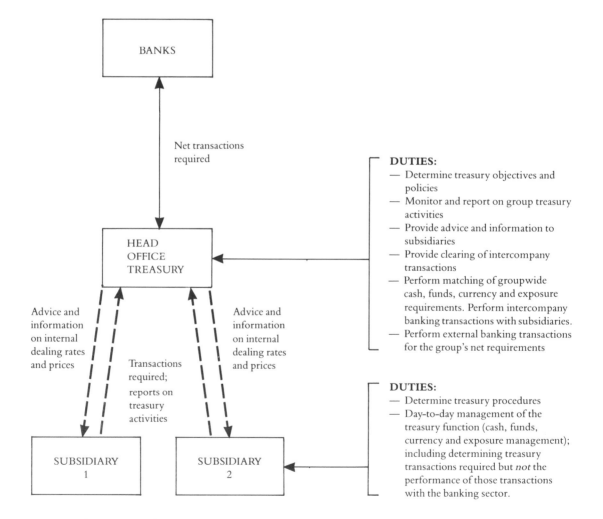

In the example given, the head office treasury provides advice and information on internal dealing rates and prices to the subsidiaries which determine the transactions required and deal with the head office treasury as though they were the subsidiaries' external bankers. The head office treasury manages the requirements of the group as a whole and negotiates with the banks on behalf of the group.

There are many treasury management techniques which the head office may apply. Several of these have been discussed in detail in Volume I, Chapter 11.

The example given is very simple indeed, but it is not difficult to visualise that if a number of currencies and subsidiaries were involved, then the number of funds transfers required would be significantly reduced. If, additionally, different currencies were offset at agreed exchange rates, then the number of funds transfers and foreign exchange contracts required would be reduced still further.

- **Matching of total group cashflows** This is the same procedure as described above except that all of the group's cashflows are included. The netting is not restricted to intragroup cashflows and includes external cashflows with third parties. Therefore the benefits, as well as the administration costs, may be very much greater
- **Leading and lagging of receivables and payables** The head office is often in a position to advise subsidiaries on how the timing of invoicing or making payments could potentially be altered to allow improved matching techniques
- **Currency of invoicing** The head office can advise subsidiaries of internal preferences for particular currencies in which to invoice. Such advice could, for instance, aid the subsidiary who is making a tender to offer a more competitive price.

As will be appreciated, in order for a group treasury to fulfil the functions described above, fairly sophisticated treasury systems will need to be in place. In Chapter 4 of this volume the operations and structures of 'Multicurrency Management Centres' which meet these requirements are discussed in detail.

The major benefits from the functions described above are the reduction in bank clearing costs and float delays, and the saving of the bank's spread on foreign exchange contracts performed internally. However, against these benefits are the additional administrative costs. Also the transfer pricing policies of the group applied in setting internal dealing rates will contribute to the acceptance and success of the processes described.

'In-house banks'

As well as the above, some of the larger companies are now forming their own 'in-house banks'. One of the first to do this was The British Petroleum Company, plc with the formation of BP Finance International.

These 'in-house banks' often have their own foreign exchange and money markets dealing rooms which service the company's requirements and are structured and operated in a similar manner to the dealing room of a bank.

Also, many of the larger companies have begun recently to issue their own Eurobonds and to perform their own syndications and obtaining commitments from banks. Although this degree of disintermediation is rather disturbing for the banking sector, at least there are not many companies with the necessary ingredients to bypass banks in this way - expertise, size, high credit-rating, low gearing and an 'in-house bank'.

Assessing the costs and benefits of the various roles

In considering a change in the role of the group treasury function, an attempt should be made to assess, and quantify wherever possible, the costs and benefits of the options available. It is wise for the role of the group treasury function to be periodically reviewed and subjected to such an evaluation.

Some of the particular costs and benefits of each of the roles are discussed below:

Advisory role

A centralised information and advisory service avoids duplication of the need to collect and analyse information at each treasury centre. Also, a higher degree of expertise and more sophisticated manual and computerised decision-support systems can be justified to service the group as a whole than just one treasury centre. This increased expertise may result in more informed negotiations between the treasury centres and the banks and could therefore be reflected in more favourable quotations received. Consistency within the group of market interpretations should also be improved.

31

Although it is only a crude calculation, the magnitude of a benefit obtained through receiving more favourable quotations should be calculated. Such a calculation can often reveal large savings.

For example, for a group with short-term borrowings of $50 million (with an average duration of three months), which expects to save ⅛% on the interest rate through the introduction of a centralised advisory function, the following annual savings would result:

$$\$50 \text{ million} \times [\ 1 + (\tfrac{1}{8}\% \times 3/12 \text{ months})^{4*}] - \$50 \text{ million}$$
$$= \$62,500 \text{ annual saving}$$

*The exponent of 4 is the reciprocal of 3/12 months to give the
number of times per annum that interest is compounded.

Likewise, a similar calculation should be made for improvements in foreign exchange rate quotations. This is done by comparing the base currency equivalents of the annual foreign currency cashflows at the exchange rates expected to be obtained with the aid of a centralised advisory function with those rates which would be obtained without such a function.

For example, assuming annual US dollar cashflows inwards of $10 million, a sterling base currency and an expected improvement in the exchange rate quotation from $1.42 to $1.40, then the following savings result:

$10 million at $1.40 = £7,142,857
$10 million at $1.42 = £7,042,254

Annual saving - £1,006,035

As stated, these are crude calculations which are not intended to be precise, but do give an idea of the magnitude of potential savings, against which to offset increased costs associated with the proposed change.

Agency role

Centralising the dealing function as well as the advisory function should result in improved expertise in dealing. An attempt should be made to quantify this benefit in a similar manner to that described above for the advisory role. The centralisation of the dealing function should also enable controls over dealing activity to be strengthened, which is more difficult to quantify. Additionally, by concentrating the dealing through the head office treasury, the group may benefit from an improved perceived presence in the markets.

Banking role

As well as generating the same benefits as the agency role, the banking role also results in a saving on bank spreads, margins, fees and charges to the extent that banking transactions are brought 'in-house' (or avoided altogether). For example, assume a matching of a $10 million cashflow inwards of one company in the group with a $10 million cashflow outwards requirement of another when a bank quotation for this amount would have been $1.4000/50.

The internal matching of these two currency requirements obviates the need for foreign exchange contracts with a bank, thereby saving the value of the bank's spread (1.4050 - 1.4000 = 50 points) which is worth:

$10 million at $1.4000 = £7,142,857
$10 million at $1.4050 = £7,117,438

Saving on bank's spread £ 25,419

In addition to the above considerations, the effect on the administrative costs must be assessed. This will involve valuation of the effect on staff costs; on data processing costs including operational, system design, implementation, hardware and software costs; on the costs of changes required to management information systems; and other changes in administrative arrangements.

Impact on treasury reporting

It is important that the reporting of treasury performance shows the performance measurement in the management accounts of the operating unit to which the decision responsibility attaches. The key factors to ensure this are the policies governing transfer pricing and intercompany management charges.

Treasury transfer prices are the prices, exchange rates and interest rates at which intercompany transactions take place. It is important that these be set at levels which encourage treasury centres to make decisions which are in the best interests of the group. Examples of this principal are:

- In the agency role structure in Figure 3.2, shown earlier in this chapter, the decision to perform a transaction is taken at treasury centre level and the transaction is performed by the head office treasury. Therefore, the rates used in the treasury management accounts of the treasury centres (that is, the 'transfer price') must not be less favourable than the rate which the treasury centre could have obtained by trading directly with a bank; otherwise there is an incentive for the treasury centre not to use the in-house agency. If need be, the transfer price used in the treasury centre's treasury reporting package could even be more favourable than the rate actually obtained with the 'loss' between the two rates being reflected in the head office treasury reporting package. However, this should be an exceptional occurrence, for example, when there is a separate reason to trade with a particular bank whose quotations are not the most favourable available
- The allocation in treasury reports of a bank spread saved by performing an in-house matching of requirements must be done by transfer prices which are within the spread of rates which could have been obtained from a bank. For example, the in-house match saving quantified above used the quotation $1.4000/50. In this case each of the two treasury centres must be quoted an internal rate of no less than $1.4000 and no greater than $1.4050
- In an advisory role, the treasury transfer prices would need to be set in order to ensure that group costs are passed on to subsidiaries but are not allocated in a manner which discourages use by a subsidiary of the group's expertise. Also, there should be a system for preparing consolidated group-wide treasury reports to enable group-wide exposures and treasury activities to be identified
- As with transfer prices (or internal dealing rates), it is important that management charges made by the group treasury to the treasury centres are set so as to ensure that treasury decision-making is not distorted, and that savings and losses arising from decisions are allocated to the department responsible for the decisions.

Key action points

The key action points for a group's treasury function to arise from this chapter are:

- Assess whether the treasury department should be a profit or a cost centre. Whatever the decision, the treasury department should have a clear set of policy guidelines agreed by the board.
- Periodically, every treasury function should review the role of its head office treasury function and whether this is continuing to be the most appropriate.
- Consider the applicability of the different forms of centralisation to the treasury function as a whole or particular treasury activities as appropriate.
- In evaluating the implications of a change in the role of a treasury function, attempts should be made to quantify costs and benefits wherever possible.
- Particular attention must be paid to determining policies regarding the setting of treasury transfer prices (internal dealing rates) and management charges in order to ensure that decisions made are in the best interests of the group as a whole.

CHAPTER 4

Multicurrency management centre operations

The increasing trend towards greater centralisation which has been discussed earlier in this volume, has led to the development of multicurrency management centres. These centres provide companies with centralised management of their funds and finance balances and of 'in-house clearing' facilities for the matching and netting of currency cashflows, thereby reducing the number of external banking transactions required.

Multicurrency Management Centre (MMC) is the term for a centralised multicurrency treasury function formed for the purposes of profitably managing treasury currency cashflow and balances. The objectives of an MMC include achieving the most effective application of worldwide cash transmission, minimising regional and worldwide borrowing costs, maximising regional and worldwide interest yields, monitoring and controlling regional and worldwide exposure to fluctuations in interest and foreign exchange rates, and acting as an adviser on treasury activities to the rest of the organisation.

These objectives imply that the MMC is a profit centre rather than a cost centre, with funds being treated as another product line. On this basis an MMC should be set up when the combined tax and commercial benefits outweigh the costs of setting up, staffing and systems and administration. This position should be contrasted with the centralised treasury set up as a cost centre, whose principal objective is to protect the company from interest and currency exposure rather than to generate profits.

This chapter considers the location and operation of MMCs, reinvoicing centres and export finance vehicles and discusses the transition from a decentralised to a centralised treasury function.

Multicurrency management centres

These are currency handling centres established by multinational companies to centralise the management and control of currency cashflows and balances. A multicurrency management centre has a number of advantages for a company in terms of increased control over currency flows and funding and exposure management.

Figure 4.1 shows the operations of a multicurrency management centre in Switzerland for a company with European and US subsidiaries. The MMC handles the currency positions of the subsidiary companies and only the MMC deals with external financial institutions.

An important function of an MMC is to exercise strict control over international payments in order to plan and control effectively the liquidity of the group. The centre would be able to channel funds to those companies with the greatest need or where borrowing costs are highest.

An MMC can be used to pool the exchange risks in one location and remove all risk from subsidiary companies. The MMC takes the local currencies payables and receivables onto its own book and becomes the sole area of foreign exchange risk for the group. The MMC can then execute foreign exchange transactions at the lowest possible cost by amalgamating the subsidiaries' positions to deal in optimum amounts. The MMC will also employ professional dealing staff who will make the transactions whereas the subsidiaries would not have this level of dealing expertise.

Figure 4.1 The operation of a multicurrency management centre

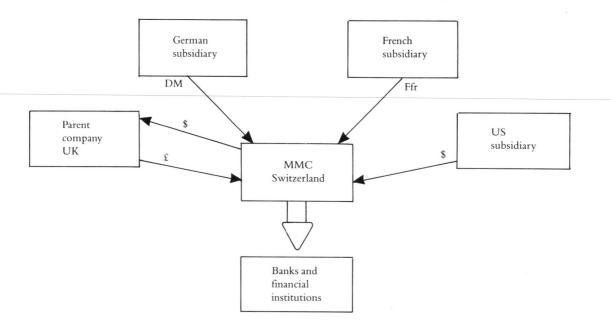

The MMC can be used to facilitate internal foreign exchange hedging techniques such as matching, netting, or leading and lagging because all the currency flows are being centralised. All these hedging techniques require a centralised management operation and the MMC is the perfect vehicle for this. Internal hedging techniques are discussed in detail in Volume I, Chapter 11.

An MMC can be used as a funding vehicle for the group by using the Eurocurrency markets for both long and short-term borrowings. The funds are borrowed by the MMC and then passed to the area of the group where they are needed. Familiarity and expertise in the Eurocurrency markets can be concentrated in the MMC and used by the whole group.

As a borrowing vehicle the MMC will have a balance sheet with liabilities of external borrowings and assets of internal lendings. The MMC is in a position to manage the group's debt in terms of maturity profile, interest cost and market spread.

Benefits of operating a multicurrency management centre

The commercial benefits from an MMC arise from reduced transaction costs and float time associated with cash collections and payments and from increased control over funds moving through the banking system. Centralised monitoring of worldwide bank services and costs means that the corporation's use of banks is more effective. There is scope for more effective investment of surplus funds by placing amounts for longer-terms with higher yields or 'playing the yield curve'.

Where treasury activities are centralised, investment and financing activities can be co-ordinated. This avoids the type of situation in which, for example, subsidiary A holds Deutschemark investments and subsidiary B has Deutschemark bank financing. Transaction sizes are normally larger so that those operating the MMC can obtain more competitive quotes for investment, finance, currency or hedge transactions.

Another advantage of an MMC is that there is often more flexibility in the use of financing instruments, cheaper access to third party finance, and better awareness of new financing techniques and costs. More instruments can be used to protect the company from interest and currency fluctuations and currencies can be offset or matched thus reducing exposure as well as dealing spreads and transactions costs.

Often overlooked is the unquantifiable benefit of greater control of investments, finance and currency exposure. These benefits usually become obvious only after lack of such control has resulted in a loss.

MMCs are not the same as reinvoicing centres, which act as intermediaries between manufacturing subsidiaries and sales subsidiaries or third parties. Reinvoicing centres purchase from the manufacturing subsidiaries at one price and sell to the sales subsidiaries or third parties at another giving rise to benefits from reduced taxation and centralisation of foreign currency dealing.

Setting up a multicurrency management centre

It will be apparent from the above that were such a concept to be considered, this could perhaps be combined with an international group financing company. However, the following points should be borne in mind:

- It has been estimated that such a centre is unlikely to be profitable unless it handles at least $50 million of invoices per annum
- Initially at least two people would be required to run such an operation, namely a foreign exchange specialist and an administrative assistant. As the role of the MMC expands, so the personnel would be increased
- Such a centre should be remunerated for its services on an arm's-length basis - either by adding a small mark-up on its billings to the sales company or alternatively charging a commission to the group company on whose behalf it bears the exchange risk
- Consequently, from an operating viewpoint, the centre should cover its costs and have a small profit margin. Any additional profit or loss will arise from exchange transactions but a problem would arise were the centre to incur an overall exchange loss in obtaining a tax deduction for such a loss
- A location should be chosen with minimal or at least flexible exchange controls permitting the use of non-resident bank accounts. As it can be appreciated, this possibility involves a number of commercial considerations and should not be considered for tax planning reasons only.

Tax planning considerations

Tax planning is an important consideration when establishing an MMC and, to a large extent, the location of the entity is dictated by tax considerations. The prime tax objectives of an MMC centre would be:

- Minimisation of taxes on exchange profits while obtaining a tax deduction for exchange losses
- Low taxes on reinvoicing fees, debt factoring discounts and interest earned
- Recovery of the MMC's costs on a tax deductible basis
- Indirect taxation status (for example, in the United Kingdom, the VAT status of the operation)
- In addition, the centre must be capable of transferring funds freely without any exchange control restrictions.

Some possible locations for MMCs are detailed in Appendix 4.1 but the possible structures which would satisfy these requirements include:

- MMC company in low tax jurisdiction, which is also a politically and economically stable location, is free from exchange controls and has tax treaties to reduce interest withholding taxes at source. This structure is advantageous if exchange profits are generated but does not enable any substantial relief to be obtained for exchange losses (because of the low rates). A common location is Switzerland, as discussed in Appendix 4.1.
  Other locations to be considered would be the Channel Islands or Caribbean havens.
- MMC company in an operating country (such as the Netherlands) where if exchange losses are realised, relief may be obtained through tax consolidation of all local group companies' results including the MMC. Full taxes are paid on exchange profits
- MMC is operated as a branch of a group company, with a head office in say the United Kingdom or the United States, where branch exchange losses could be relieved against head office profits. Exchange gains would be taxable at normal rates in the country where the MMC is established. Although possible, this structure does not tend to be used in practice
- The use of an MMC established by the parent company or independent bank to manage the foreign currency transactions of all foreign subsidiaries under the auspices of a pooling agreement. The MMC is not a separate company but exchange profits/losses and MMC costs are pooled and reallocated to each foreign subsidiary on the bases of transactions handled.

The MMC must be remunerated on an 'arm's-length' basis and should charge a fee for its services plus a reasonable mark-up. This can be accomplished by adding a small mark-up to invoices which are rebilled in a local currency or the MMC could charge each subsidiary company participating in the scheme, a service fee based on the sales put through the MMC. A figure which has been used in practice is 0.4% of sales. This is comprised as follows:

- 0.25% for credit and exchange risk
- 0.15% for collection costs.

Provided it can be shown that a subsidiary benefits from the scheme and the fee is in line with that payable to an outside bank then it should be tax deductible to the local subsidiary, although tax chargeable to the MMC. Where payments are made to an MMC in a low tax jurisdiction the tax authorities in the various countries would probably require more justification and substantiation of the fees payable before they will be accepted as tax deductible.

Tax authorities would not generally accept an allocation of an MMC's exchange losses to local subsidiaries in addition to paying service fees for transfer of credit and exchange risk.

In the case of the scheme which involves pooling of exchange profits and losses, the reallocation of the results of the MMC to subsidiaries is more likely to be acceptable to local tax authorities provided the resulting exchange losses and costs do not exceed those which would have been borne by the company if it had taken its own risk or alternatively engaged an independent bank to carry out a similar function for a fee.

Reinvoicing centres

Figure 4.2: Currency exposure centralisation through a reinvoicing centre

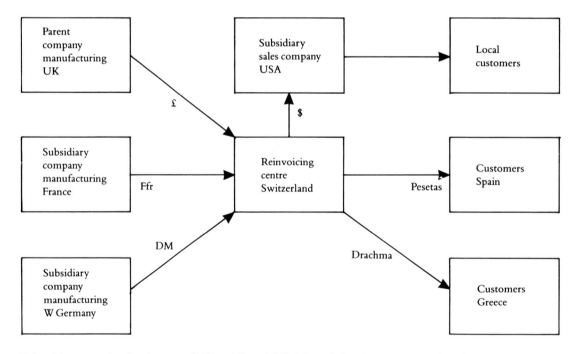

Reinvoicing centre showing the route of billing. All goods billed through the reinvoicing centre flow directly from the manufacturer to the purchaser.

A reinvoicing centre is a vehicle through which intercompany and third party invoices are routed.

Goods exported from a subsidiary company are shipped directly either to a subsidiary or third party customer, but the invoice (and therefore payment) is passed through the reinvoicing centre. Transactional exposures can be centralised by invoicing subsidiary companies in their local currencies. This centralisation facilitates internal exposure management by the application of techniques such as matching, netting or leading and lagging. The principal benefits of a reinvoicing centre are:

38

- Exposure is centralised in one location where information and expertise can also be concentrated. Hedging opportunities are also centralised
- Liquidity is concentrated at the reinvoicing centre creating a larger pool of funds to be invested at optimum rates
- The costs of transactions are reduced as the centre is able to deal in larger size and with greater expertise.

Figure 4.2 shows how a Swiss reinvoicing centre operates for a UK company with European and US subsidiaries. All invoices are passed through the centre which then invoices the customers.

In order to warrant the establishment of a reinvoicing centre, a company must have a substantial volume of intercompany and third party trade. As with an MMC, it is estimated that a reinvoicing centre requires annual volumes of around $50 million before it is worthwhile.

Figure 4.3 shows how the introduction of a reinvoicing centre will double the volume of trade flows within a group.

Figure 4.3: The impact of a reinvoicing centre on trade flow

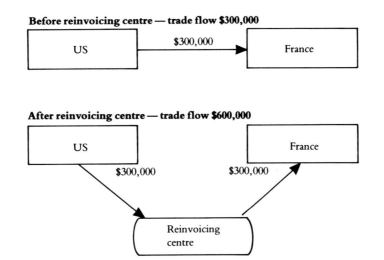

This inevitably increases administrative costs and is only feasible if benefits are obtained from reinvoicing to offset these costs, but the use of a cash management technique such as matching or netting helps to justify this expansion of trade flows.

The location of a reinvoicing centre is discussed in Appendix 4.1 but must take account of four particular factors:

- Freedom from regulatory constraints is an important feature of the location of a reinvoicing centre. The company should select a location without restrictive controls on foreign exchange, intercompany loans or external financial dealings
- The reinvoicing centre should be located in an area where tax on both income and interest and other payments is low
- The facilities available for the reinvoicing centre must be sufficient for the effective operation of the business. This means that the financial systems must be well developed; there must be a good communications network and local staff must be of a suitable calibre. These constraints eliminate many of the developing countries as potential locations for reinvoicing centres
- The nature and organisation already existing in the company will affect the location of a reinvoicing centre. It may be that the company already has interests in a particular location and would prefer to use this area for the reinvoicing centre. The company must also consider that head office management may wish to visit the reinvoicing centre and their travelling costs must be considered. It is also convenient if the centre is located in the same time zone as the head office of the company to aid communication between the two centres.

Companies may pool cash at the national level in several countries, but international pooling is difficult because of tax regulations, exchange control and the practical problems associated with creating a pool of funds denominated in different currencies.

The management of intercompany trade through a reinvoicing centre enables funds to be reallocated between previously unconnected units. If the reinvoicing centre is located in an area which is free from exchange control constraints the company can take full advantage of leading and lagging possibilities to create a central pool of liquidity which can either be used for funding purposes or invested at optimum interest rates.

Leading occurs when payments are made before their due date; lagging occurs when payments are made after their due date. The use of leading and lagging to create a liquidity pool is shown in Figure 4.4.

Figure 4.4: The impact of a reinvoicing centre on funding

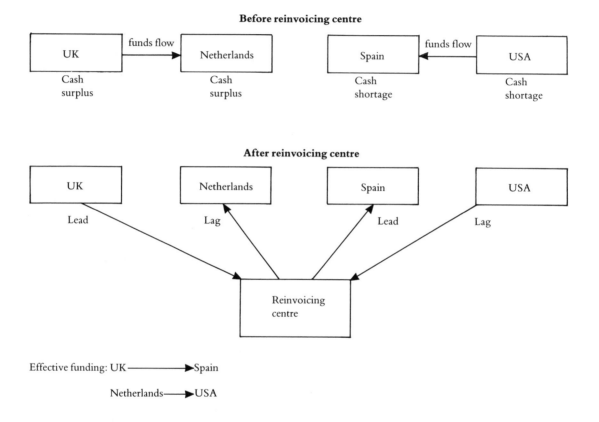

By leading and lagging payments as shown in Figure 4.4, the UK company is effectively funding the Spanish company and the Dutch company is effectively funding the US company.

The cost of establishing a reinvoicing centre can be quite high but will vary according to the location and structure of the centre. The initial costs of a reinvoicing centre can be divided into three phases:

- Phase 1 - Before the decision is taken to set up a reinvoicing centre, the company must undertake research into the feasibility of the project. Once the decision has been taken, the company will need to undertake an internal promotion to explain the rationale behind the centre and the new allocation of financial reponsibilites
- Phase 2 - After the decision has been taken, but before implementation can begin, the company will incur legal and other professional fees as it establishes the desired legal and tax structures for the centre
- Phase 3 - The implementation process will involve disruption of existing systems and a loss of effectiveness until the new system is operating efficiently. The costs of this are difficult to quantify but are an important consideration.

The running costs of a reinvoicing centre will depend largely upon the scope of the centre's activities, but these costs can be summarised as:

- Operational - including production of the invoices and maintaining the records and accounts of the centre
- Personnel - staff levels are generally low, but this depends upon the scope of activities undertaken by the centre and the level of computerisation
- Technical - these costs are dependent upon the level of computerisation and the rental costs of hardware and software.

A reinvoicing centre may need to demonstrate that it has made a profit in order to satisfy local tax authorities. Failure to do this may raise questions about tax avoidance through transfer pricing alterations within the group. The centre must not appear to be merely a vehicle for tax avoidance but must be shown to be providing a financial service to the company. For this service, the reinvoicing centre should receive a margin on each transaction.

The reinvoicing centre must not be a centre for currency speculation as this involves a risk to the company. However, it is likely that foreign exchange transactions undertaken by the centre will provide some profit due to the expertise of the traders. Despite the considerable benefits, reinvoicing centres are relatively uncommon. This is due partly to opposition from operating units to the loss of an important part of their treasury function and partly due to the considerable costs involved in running a reinvoicing centre. As with an MMC, a reinvoicing centre is only worthwhile if it can handle significant volumes of business on behalf of the group.

Export finance vehicles

An export finance vehicle buys in the export receivables of subsidiary companies for settlement in the subsidiaries' local currencies. For non-intercompany exports the operation is as follows:

- Trade transaction is invoiced as usual
- The exporting company sells the export receivable to the export finance vehicle
- At maturity, the export finance vehicle collects the receivable either directly or from the export company.

Figure 4.5: a) Export finance vehicle where exporter collects receivables

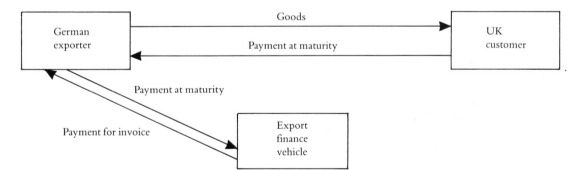

b) Export finance vehicle where vehicle collects receivables

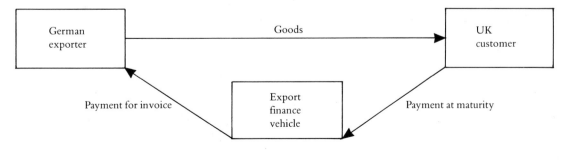

Intercompany exports are invoiced to the subsidiary in the importer's currency thereby shifting transactional exposure to the export finance vehicle.

The export finance vehicle operates as an in-house factoring company. The vehicle can either be structured to collect all the receivables for the group, or the individual companies can be responsible for collecting their own receivables and then passing the payment on to the vehicle.

Figure 4.5 shows an export finance vehicle acting between a German exporter and a UK customer. The export finance vehicle can work in two ways, either where the exporter collects the receivables or where the vehicle itself collects the receivables.

This is an attractive scheme for a company which frequently uses the services of factoring houses although the credit risk is retained within the group. The export finance vehicle will pay a price for the receivables which depends upon the risk it is taking on. This will inevitably be similar to the price which would be received from an external factoring house.

The export finance vehicle must have adequate resources to collect outstanding receivables. This may be an expensive operation as the vehicle will need to be able to function in all the countries to which the group exports.

The transition to a centralised treasury

The decision for the treasury function of a company to become 'more centralised' must be sanctioned by the main board of the company, although the idea may originate from the treasurer. Centralisation of treasury operations often meets with resistance and cannot occur unless the board supports the idea and gives the treasurer the authority to carry it through.

The process of centralisation must be gradual if it is to succeed as many operating difficulties will have to be ironed out before the system is functioning smoothly. Initially the company may decide to centralise either certain subsidiaries only, certain functions only or a combination of these two alternatives. For example:

- Centralise French and German subsidiaries only
- Centralise all subsidiaries for intercompany foreign exchange transactions only
- Centralise French and German subsidiaries for intercompany foreign exchange transactions only.

The method and speed of the centralisation process will depend largely upon the size and nature of the individual company. However, the following are general rules for centralisation:

- A reasonable timetable for centralisation should be established and adhered to wherever possible
- One individual (normally the treasurer) must have overall responsibility for the process of centralisation
- Each stage of centralisation must be properly controlled and evaluated
- Once centralisation is complete, the monitoring process should continue.

Key action points

There are several key action points for a treasury function arising from the points discussed in this chapter:

- Consider the type of treasury transactions undertaken by the company - are there high levels of intergroup trade?
- Calculate an estimate of the volumes of trade - both intergroup and third party.
- Are there techniques for hedging or currency management which are not currently being used which could be facilitated by a centralised operation? These should be taken into account in the calculation.

- Consider the applicability of different types of centralised treasury operations, for example, MMCs, reinvoicing centres and export finance vehicles.
- Review the possible geographic locations for a centralised operation.
- Estimate the costs involved in setting up and running a centralised operation.
- Decide whether centralisation could be feasible for the company.
- If a centralised operation does not seem worthwhile, keep the subject under review to be raised again.

APPENDIX 4.1

Location of an MMC or reinvoicing centre

The MMC or reinvoicing centre should preferably be located in a low tax jurisdiction which is also a stable location, is free from exchange controls and has the advantages of a good international tax treaty network.

Most European countries meet such requirements except in respect of the level of taxation, which is generally in the region of 40% to 50% and also in some cases in respect of exchange controls. Pure tax haven locations are generally not advisable for such a centre because of the attitude to them taken by the non-tax-haven fiscal authorities.

Consequently, on these criteria, Switzerland would be suitable, being a stable location, relatively free of exchange controls, having a wide treaty network and a tax rate significantly lower than that of most other European countries.

Switzerland

An MMC or reinvoicing centre in Switzerland could be structured in a number of ways.

The centre could be set up as a normal company, paying normal federal and cantonal taxes, and employing its own personnel in Switzerland. However, unless all the required personnel are Swiss residents, there may be problems in obtaining non-Swiss-resident personnel because of the difficulty of obtaining work permits. This, combined with the possibility of structuring the centre such that no or reduced cantonal taxes are payable, may not make the use of such a 'normal' company acceptable or even possible.

The tax laws of some cantons grant (or permit on arrangement) to so-called 'domiciliary companies' tax concessions similar to those accorded to holding companies. This generally involves a freedom from cantonal (and communal) income taxes but not from the small net worth taxes. A domiciliary corporation is, in general, one which (although not a holding company) maintains its legal headquarters in Switzerland, but owns no real estate and does no business therein. Within this concept fall corporations that own patents and whose income consists of foreign licence fees, and corporations that own real estate abroad or whose income (mark-ups, commissions) is derived from transactions concluded and consummated abroad and which do not touch Switzerland. As a rule, such corporations maintain their domicile with a fiduciary company or with an attorney-at-law; records are kept and administrative matters are handled in accord with the client's instructions. The applicable cantons are Appenzell AR, Neuchatel, Obwalden, Schwyz, St Gallen, Ticino, Thurgau, Unterwalden, Uri, Wallis, Zug.

Because a domicilary company is no more than a registered office, the co-ordination and administration of the operations and banking transactions can be contracted to a 'management centre' located in, for example the Netherlands.

This management centre should make a charge to the Swiss company for the services it performs. It should be possible to organise the management centre operation so that it is taxed in the Netherlands only on a percentage of costs under a special tax ruling.

Netherlands company/Swiss branch

An alternative structure that may fit better into a group's structure, particularly where withholding tax on dividends is perceived to be a problem, is a Netherlands company which carries on the MMC or reinvoicing centre activity entirely through a Swiss branch. The advantages are:

The income of the branch is taxed at the relatively lower Swiss rates which vary in the different cantons.

Generally, profits attributed to the foreign branch of a Dutch company are virtually free of Dutch tax.

The Dutch treaty network is the one applicable. It tends to be more beneficial than the Swiss network. A Swiss branch cannot use Swiss treaties because it is not resident in Switzerland. As a result anti-abuse provisions for Swiss treaty-protected income (for example, minimum distribution requirements or limitations on 'conduiting' income) do not apply. Because it is a branch, the Swiss activity is not subject to Swiss capital taxes. As a branch, it is not subject to Swiss dividend withholding tax.

The Dutch company/Swiss branch must be operated with care - both in the Netherlands and in Switzerland. Rulings from both jurisdictions should be obtained to provide certainty. For this it is necessary that:

- Both the Netherlands and Swiss operations have substance
- The Swiss branch has substantial equity.

A portion of the branch profits may be allocated by the Dutch authorities to the head office to recognise a substantial management function for the branch, with the result that such portion of the profit would be taxed in the Netherlands rather than Switzerland.

Belgium

At the end of 1982, a new regulation granting a 10-year tax holiday and other advantages to co-ordination centres was issued by the Belgian government.

Due to objections of the European Commission, co-ordination centres recognised after 27 December 1984 are not entirely tax exempt; instead they are subject to Belgian tax at 45% but only on a percentage of operating and overhead expenses excluding financing and personnel costs. The percentage is determined on a case by case basis.

Tax treaties entered into by Belgium provide for tax exemption for co-ordination offices. The government deems, however, that such tax treaty provisions are insufficient because the tax exemption is granted only to Belgian establishments of foreign companies and the activities must be limited to those set forth in the tax treaty. A further obstacle, among others, is that the Belgian social security scheme is applicable to non-Belgian executives and specialists.

The new regulation now extends the advantages for co-ordination offices to Belgian companies, provided they form part of a group and to Belgian establishments of foreign companies that are not located in a tax treaty country. Furthermore, it widens the range of activities that can be carried out by the co-ordination office. These activities are in line with the definitions of the 1977 OECD double-taxation convention model, which refers to activities that have a preparatory or auxiliary character for the enterprise, and may go beyond those stipulated in the tax treaties. Co-ordination offices may now also carry out such activities as the centralisation of financial transactions and the coverage or risks resulting from exchange rate fluctuations.

The objectives of a qualifying co-ordination centre must be restricted, solely for the benefit of all or part of the group companies, to the development and the centralisation of one or several of the following activities:

- Advertising
- Collection and supply of information
- Insurance and reinsurance
- Scientific research
- Relations with national and international authorities
- Accounting centralisation
- Administration and data processing
- Centralising of financial transactions and the coverage of risks resulting from exchange rate fluctuations
- All activities that have a preparatory and auxiliary character for the group companies.

'Group' means all of the related companies that, through direct or indirect participation by one or several of them in one of several others, are placed under one and the same management.

The advantages are granted to the centre from the day it is advised of its recognition as a qualifying co-ordination centre until 31 December of the 10th year following the year in which it was so advised. Qualifying co-ordination centres must be recognised as such by Royal Decree.

Distributed and retained profits of a co-ordination centre set up in the form of a company having its registered office, its main establishment or its seat of management in Belgium are exempt from corporate income tax.

Profits of a co-ordination centre set up in the form of a branch of a company that does not have its registered office, its main establishment, or its management seat in Belgium are totally exempt from non-resident income tax when these profits are maintained in the accounts of the Belgian establishment and are exempt to the extent of 50% when these profits are transferred to the foreign establishment of the company.

No exemption is granted on 'abnormal benevolent advantages' (non-arm's-length) that are obtained by the co-ordination centre from related entities.

CHAPTER 5

Integrated reporting systems

The greater the level of centralisation within the treasury the greater the need for fast, accurate information to be available in the treasury function. The timing of treasury decisions is most important and delays can cost money. Action to execute a foreign exchange transaction, for example, has to be done at the most appropriate moment, and cannot be delayed while the treasurer completes some analysis or obtains additional information. Therefore, of prime importance to a treasurer is an information reporting system that is not only up-to-the-minute, but is flexible enough to assist him with both the expected and the unexpected decision-making.

A treasurer does not operate independently; not only must he make decisions but also he must control the activities of his staff and communicate his department's actions to senior management. Furthermore, he must keep senior management informed of the current and projected state of the company as regards treasury matters. Therefore, in addition to supporting his decision-making, a treasurer's information reporting system must satisfy all his internal control and management reporting requirements.

A further benefit of a well defined treasury reporting system is to ease the problem of communication with senior management. This can result from a difference in orientation where senior financial managers have not served in the treasury function. If they have come through the management and financial accounting side they will be more used to dealing with historic data and long-term decisions rather than current data and short-term decisions.

We can see therefore, that a really comprehensive treasury reporting system must encompass all the activities of a treasury department. If we think in terms of the 'life' of an individual transaction, then we can categorise these activities into:

— Transaction planning or modelling

— Pre-deal procedures

— Dealing and transaction recording

— Management reporting.

An integrated reporting system must provide all the reports needed for each of these activities. The natural extension then of an integrated reporting system is an integrated treasury system, also known as the treasury workstation that is capable of satisfying not just reporting but all other requirements of each of these activities. We examine below each activity in turn and then look at the treasury workstation in terms of the systems available, the selection procedure and likely future developments.

Modelling

Modelling enables treasurers quickly and accurately to apply 'what if' analyses to their cashflow forecasts. For example, what is the net exposed position if my US dollar balances decline by 10% or my Deutschemark balances rise by 15%? What is my cleared cash position by the end of today? Modelling also helps treasurers to evaluate and analyse the costs and benefits of placing alternative investment tranches or raising alternative financing packages - perhaps contrasting the net present value of a five-year loan with equal interest and capital repayments and a bullet loan with a six-month interest moratorium.

A modelling package enables a treasurer to assess the vulnerability of his position to changes in interest or exchange rates. It is important that the modelling package functions quickly and easily otherwise it will not be used. The treasurer needs fast answers to his queries as a slow response may be too late.

The modelling package can be used to provide useful information for presentation to the board at treasury policy meetings. Rather than the treasurer saying, 'We will suffer higher interest costs if US interest rates rise', he can say: 'It will cost the company an additional $500,000 per annum in interest costs if US interest rates rise to 12% and an additional $700,000 if they rise to 12½%'. This type of information would be time consuming to produce manually but a modelling package can produce it within seconds.

Pre and post deal support requirements

Before a treasurer decides to make a foreign exchange or money market transaction, he needs information to help him formulate his decision. This information is both internal and external in origin and helps the treasurer to relate his position to the external environment.

Internal information

The first internal information requirement is an accurate rolling cashflow forecast. This can be, say, three or 12 months in outlook and is regularly updated. The cashflow forecast shows the next three or 12 months' cashflow regardless of the calendar or financial year-end. Input to the cashflow forecast is from all the divisions and subsidiaries of the group and the need for accuracy is paramount. Members of either the finance or treasury departments must have responsibility for comparing the forecast figures to the actual cashflows and querying discrepancies with the divisions responsible. The individuals with overall responsibility for the cashflow forecast must have the authority to ensure that standards of accuracy are high. The cashflow forecast must be analysed by currency with totals by currency and in the base currency. Translation to base currency must be based on the most recent forecast of expected exchange rates.

The rolling cashflow forecast gives an outlook of the expected cash position for the next period. From this can be extracted a daily forecast position which will take the form of a diary showing all known and forecast cashflows.

The treasurer cannot identify his dealing requirements without accurate forecast information. For example, a treasurer with inadequate information may know that he will receive DM2 million the following week and decide to sell the DMs for his base currency; however, if the treasurer had accurate forecast information he would also know that he has a requirement for DM2 million in two weeks' time. With full information this treasurer would be able to identify the opportunity to match these flows, making a foreign exchange transaction unnecessary.

External information

Apart from knowledge of the internal position, a treasurer also requires external information before he can deal. This takes the form of current and forecast market information. Current information is available on-line from suppliers such as Reuters or Telerate which provide news, market reports and up-to-date rate information.

The only other means of obtaining this information is by telephone or telex from banks. This is slow, time consuming and limited as bank dealers do not have the resources to provide an information service to their corporate clients.

The on-line information services enable subscribers to view their chosen pages at any time and as the information is collected from a large number of banks, it is a market view rather than just one bank's position.

Forecast market information can be obtained from a number of sources. The cheapest source is the economics department of a lead bank which can provide high quality information both in printed form and over the telephone. Subscriber services vary in price and type but most services are either printed and updated by telex, or on-line and updated automatically. A treasurer subscribing to such a service should monitor results properly to ensure that he is getting value for money.

Dealing support information

Once the treasurer has decided to deal, he needs immediate information about his current position in the market. This would include:

- The recent deal profile by bank - which deals have been done with each bank. This is to ensure a spread of transactions among authorised banks
- Bank limits - this compares the deals outstanding with each bank to the bank's limits as laid down by the board. By this means the treasurer can ensure that dealing limits are not exceeded
- Bank's performance - some companies employ a measure of the rates quoted by their banks so that consistently unhelpful banks can be dropped from the authorised dealing list
- Maturity profile by currency - in the case of money market transactions it is generally advisable to maintain a spread of maturities to avoid being unduly affected by adverse market conditions which may arise on any particular day.

A company will require a database of its own selected information. This may include:

- The names, addresses and telephone numbers of the banks along with the current contact name for each type of business. For example:

XYZ Bank
15 New Street

Telephone: 0439 72163

Account Officer: [Name]
FX Dealer: [Name]
Money Market Dealer: [Name]

- Details of relationship banks for all types of business in the whole group. Many companies like to consolidate their positions with banks which are providing a service in other areas by using them for foreign exchange and money market transactions

- Dealing limits. These should be laid down by the board and may comprise:

  - Limits by amount for each company dealer
  - Limits by currency for each company dealer
  - Limits for each bank
  - Limits on individual deal size.

While a deal is being made over the telephone, the dealer should record the details of the transaction and agree these with the other party. Most dealers complete a dealing slip which provides a permanent paper record of the deal and can be consulted in the case of a query.

From the dealing slip, the company's records can be updated and a confirmation letter can be produced. The information on the dealing slip is used to update the records of both the treasury and the accounts department whether or not these departments have a common database. The confirmation letter contains the same information as the dealing slip and is produced in a format which is standard to the company. The confirmation letter is signed by the company's authorised signatories and is then mailed to the counterparty.

The treasurer requires a constant overview of his position, updated to show the most recent transactions. It is important that the information for each transaction is quickly transferred to the company's records to appear on the treasurer's database. Each transaction must be recorded in terms of:

- Date of deal
- Type of deal
- Counterparty name
- Maturity date
- Amount
- Currencies
- Interest/exchange rate
- Payment instructions
- Dealer's name
- Counterparty dealer's name
- The purpose of the transaction, for example: 'Sale of $ Dividend', 'Purchase of French francs for loan to French subsidiary'.

The treasurer needs a flexible database which will enable him to view his position in terms of a number of different criteria. Some of these criteria are particular to individual companies, but include:

- Currency
- Deal size
- Deal date
- Maturity date
- Counterparty
- Dealer
- Interest/exchange rate.

It is necessary to monitor forward foreign exchange transactions to determine the gains and losses on exchange arising on each one. This information is used to decide when a contract should be closed out to take either a loss or profit on the currency.

The treasury department must have a report of its exposed currency position to enable exposure to be monitored and controlled and to allow informed hedging decisions to be taken.

Many treasury departments calculate some measure of their own performance in terms of the foreign exchange and money market transactions which they make. This is normally done by comparing the actual rates achieved with some sort of 'standard' rate ruling on that day.

Management reporting requirements

Management reporting systems enable treasurers to communicate to financial management the actions they are undertaking and help financial management to monitor and control the activities of the treasury function. Reports might be prepared monthly covering movements, balances and performance for transactions associated with placing investments, raising finance and executing currency spot and hedge transactions.

The board or exposure committee will wish to review periodically the forecast information on which the treasury department is currently basing its decisions. This is the internal cashflow forecast information and the external market information which the treasurer receives. Senior management will probably require only a short version of the cashflow forecast and a resume of the external forecast information.

Reports showing gains and losses on forward foreign exchange contracts will be used by management when assessing the currency exposure of the group and when deciding on a target exchange rate at which option contracts should be exercised.

The management reporting requirements vary from one company to another. In some instances, management want to review very detailed information regarding both historical and future treasury decisions; in other companies the treasurer is given more authority and management will only review summary reports. Nevertheless, the following general principles should be applied in developing a management reporting system:

- Conformity to the required objectives of management in terms of data to be reported, format, frequency and destination of distribution
- Pyramid reporting. The reports should form a pyramid or hierarchy of different levels of detail, the more detailed reporting levels forming input to less detailed levels

- Exception reporting. To avoid excess data, reporting by exception should be followed wherever applicable. A set of exception criteria should be established and reports produced only when these are breached.

A suggested list of reports with frequency and destination is given as Figure 5.1. This list includes reports to identify exposure, to assist in evaluating alternative treasury actions, to summarise and report on treasury activities and to report exceptional events to management. This reporting package incorporates some selected performance measures.

Balance reporting

In the late 1960's, corporate demand for balance reporting was the prime user requirement behind the development of cash management systems. Now corporate treasurers based in London, for example, can maintain dollar bank accounts in New York or Deutschemark accounts in Frankfurt, and can monitor and control the balances on those accounts through desktop terminals. They can in this way control non-interest bearing accounts or arbitrage investment returns between US investments or Eurodollar placements.

Balance reporting services have four main variables: the level of detail, the format of the page delivered, the time horizon of information and the frequency of update.

Balance report information is built up in a pyramid of levels of detail. At the top of the pyramid is typically a listing of balances by currency and by account. The next level of detail breaks down the account balance into a listing of deposits and payments which have moved across the account to provide that balance. Further detail, such as paying bank and currency of receipt and subsequent conversion, is then available for individual deposits or payments.

Levels of detail tend to be similar for all banks but the page format in which the data are delivered varies and can be more or less useful to recipients. For treasurers, the most desirable length of time covered by each page depends on how far back they want information on balances, and how much detail they need on forward clearing.

At present, most systems are updated on a batch basis at specific times during the day. The frequency of updates varies between banks, and there is now some debate among corporate treasurers about the need for real-time balance reporting. The latest available information is useful for treasurers needing to know that they are in funds, and therefore matched before initiating large payments. But it is questionable whether real-time balance reporting has much value for monitoring and control, which are undertaken at specific times during the day rather than continually.

Most cash management systems provide cleared balances as at the close of business on the previous day. However, the closing balance at the end of day one may differ from the opening balance on day two, because of items which were passed on day one or earlier but with value on day two, such as cheques. Cash management systems with frequent updating can provide, first thing on day two, day one closing balances already updated with clearing for day two. The benefits of computerised balance reporting systems are that they provide information which enables treasurers to minimise the existence of idle, non-interest bearing balances, or to move balances from lower to higher interest accounts. Mismatches of currency receipts and payments can be monitored, and committed foreign currency exposure can be managed. Cash receipts can be controlled by ensuring that they have arrived in the right amount, currency, time and place. Bank charges can be more easily equated with transaction levels and the reconciliation process between bank ledger and cash positions can be eased, particularly through the identification of value dates of transactions.

Apart from tighter controls, these benefits result in real cash savings. Float delays, calculated as 38c per $1,000 per interest day at 10%, can be eliminated, bank charges can be minimised and labour intensive administrative functions can be streamlined.

Figure 5.1: Summary specification of treasury reporting system

Category within Reporting System	Type/Name of Report	Frequency of Preparation	Distribution Within Treasury	Distribution Outside Treasury
1 FORECASTS TO IDENTIFY SITUATIONS	CASHFLOW FORECASTS:			
	(1) Long-term cashflow *	As required	X	X
	(2) 12 and three-month rolling cashflow forecast	Monthly and weekly	X	X
	(3) Daily cash position estimate	Daily	X	–
	(4) Treasury plan	Quarterly	X	X
2 FRAMEWORKS TO LIST AND EVALUATE OPTIONS	OPTION LISTS FOR:			
	(1) Short-term investments	As required	By request	By request
	(2) Short-term financing			
	(3) Hedging techniques			
	WORKSHEETS TO EVALUATE ALTERNATIVE:			
	(1) Short-term investments	As required	By request	–
	(2) Short-term financing			–
	(3) Hedging techniques			
3 REPORTS TO RECORD, MONITOR AND CONTROL ACTIVITIES	SUMMARY REPORTS:			
	Investing cash:			
	(1) Daily investment summary	Daily	X	–
	(2) Monthly investment report	Monthly	X	X
	Funding cash requirements:			
	(1) Daily funding summary	Daily	X	–
	(2) Monthly funding report	Monthly	X	X
	Foreign exchange transactions:			
	(1) Daily foreign exchange summary	Daily	X	–
	(2) Monthly foreign exchange report	Monthly	X	X
	Exposure management:			
	(1) Daily forward exchange contract summary	Daily	X	–
	(2) Monthly forward exchange contract report	Monthly	X	X
	(3) Internal hedging report	Quarterly	X	X
	Banking/counterparty:			
	(1) Counterparty business analysis report	Quarterly	X	X
	(2) Transaction confirmation slip	As required	By request	–
4 REPORTS TO WARN MANAGEMENT	EXCEPTION REPORTS FOR:			
	(1) Short-term investments	As required	X	X
	(2) Short-term financing		X	X
	(3) Foreign exchange transactions		X	X
	(4) Hedging transactions			

* Not included in package

How to choose a balance reporting system

The choice of balance reporting systems is complex and Appendix 5.1 gives a checklist of the requirements which could form the basis of an evaluation. However, before treasurers decide to choose any service at all, they should be clear about the answers to several questions:

- How is the information required? By mail, telex, terminal, phone or Reuter Monitor?
- What level of detail is required? Balance only, balance and transaction, or fully detailed transaction data?
- Which information is required? Prior day's, today's, ledger, cleared and available, historical, or forecast?
- How often is this information required? Intraday, daily, weekly, or monthly?

When these questions have been answered, treasurers can evaluate the available services, concentrating on a number of key factors:

- **Bank relations**: The user should be able to retain flexibility in bank relations and not be required to place transfer and foreign exchange business through the bank. Such business should normally be placed on a competitive and performance related basis
- **Cleared available balances**: Balances should incorporate current day credit clearing and be reported as cleared and therefore available in addition to entries which are still subject to value dating delay. As the table shows, most services give current previous day balances and indicate value date transactions. However, there are differences in the systems' ability to identify clearing items. Some systems can identify items clearing as much as five days ahead; however, the norm seems to be three days
- **Access to non-vendor banks**: The cash management system should be able to receive and report non-vendor bank account balances. If it cannot, the customer is locked into the vendor and its correspondent banks or has to use the balance reporting systems of several banks, with the inconvenience of different passwords, formats and procedures
- **Control facilities**: The funds transfer services should have adequate control facilities and the balance reporting system should be able to report information in a format and level of detail that allows the user to monitor accounts effectively
- **Method of operation**: The system should be as simple as possible to operate. Some systems have a series of menus within menus; others can be operated by accessing command codes
- **Frequency of update**: Treasurers should work out how frequently they wish information to be updated. Most systems can update at least daily whereas others are able to give some information on a real-time basis
- **Level of detail required**: Some systems can produce a summary schedule of transactions by type. In addition, some can also provide back-up data for items by account and by transaction
- **System enhancements**: These should be considered in relation to the needs of the corporate treasury. Such enhancements include sensitivity analysis to cashflow forecasts driven by the balance reports, market commentary, exposure management, interest reapportionment, or treasury reporting modules.

Electronic funds transfer

The terminal of the cash management system is a means of communicating international and domestic funds transfer instructions to the bank. In most cases, transfer payaway instructions can be loaded into the system and, with appropriate security measures, can be initiated as required.

Over the past year, funds transfer capability has developed rapidly and some systems can now initiate the payment of urgent cheques, letters of credit or securities transactions.

Electronic transaction initiation enables treasurers to use or move available funds more quickly, thus reducing idle balances. Transactions can be initiated with greater control and accuracy than with manual methods and there can be cost savings over the manual administration of transactions. Many treasurers worry that electronic funds transfer is open to fraud, or that they will not be able to maintain control over payment.

Inclusion of non-vendor banks

Criticisms of early balance reporting facilities focused on their inability to supply information from third party banks. Treasurers feared that by adopting a cash management system from one bank, they would be forced to keep all their accounts with that bank. While the banks may have welcomed such moves, they have recognised the need to expand their reporting services to include other banks and have responded in various ways.

Now, systems are able to obtain information from banks which are not branches of the bank supplying the cash management system. These institutions are termed non-vendor banks. The non-vendor banks supply information to a 'data pool'.

The usefulness of these pooled systems hinges on the extent to which non-vendor banks are prepared to provide information. For banks which are willing to participate, the SWIFT 940 message format enables data to be submitted in the required format. SWIFT - the Society for Worldwide Interbank Financial Telecommunication - is likely to become increasingly involved in providing information to pooled systems as banks and corporations accept the need for standardised electronic reporting.

The main disadvantage of the pooling networks is that they normally provide only the previous day's cleared balances and statements from the other banks together with transaction details. If intraday balances are required, customers must go through the branches which hold their accounts. With their on-line communications to CHIPS (the US Clearing House Interbank Payments System), CHAPS (the UK Clearing House Automated Payments System), or SWIFT, branch information is updated virtually on a real-time basis.

A further problem is that funds transfer cannot be initiated through the pooled systems. The leading banks are now refining their funds transfer capability and corporate treasurers may soon be able to use the networks for transaction initiation, for example, when their own banks are closed but transactions are needed for other time zones.

System enhancements

Add-on modules have upgraded cash management systems to provide treasurers with decision-making support, including word processing, spreadsheet, information database and graphics capability.

These systems enable treasurers to undertake projections of daily funding requirements in, for example, dollars, sterling and other currencies. Updated balances obtained at 8.30 am, can be automatically input to create a cash position estimate for the day or, for example, a 30-day rolling cashflow forecast by currency. These forecasts can then be stored on disk for comparison against actual movements.

Systems are being developed which can accept manually input transaction and counterparty limits and maintain cumulative positions against these as deals are executed.

To provide support for foreign exchange deals, the systems will be able to log details of spot or forward transactions and to form a currency transaction database. These logs could be used to generate open position reports and using bank rates, to revalue forward positions.

Other modules available for cash management systems cater for reinvoicing, multilateral netting, bilateral netting, foreign currency exposure management, forward contract tracking, foreign currency and money market commentary and forecasting, and daily rates, with analysis and graphing tools.

These developments are taking cash management services increasingly into the areas covered by treasury workstations and indicating that, in future, banks wishing to maintain leading positions in electronic banking may have to devote more time to software development and less to the straightforward supply of information.

The treasury workstation

A treasury workstation is most clearly defined as 'an integrated computerised treasury system which brings together in one workstation the information, decision support, transaction processing and control and management reporting sub-systems required to operate the treasury function'.

User requirements for modelling, pre-deal and post-deal support and management reporting can be translated into inputs, functions and outputs for the treasury workstation. This is illustrated by Figure 5.2. Inputs include bank balance reports, cashflow forecasts, and information on interest and exchange rates and prices of securities, gilts etc as appropriate. Functions of the workstation include modelling for planning and cost/benefit analysis; transaction processing for controlling, recording and accounting; and reporting for analysing and monitoring. The outputs of the workstation are pre-deal and post-deal support and treasury reporting.

Figure 5.2: The treasury workstation

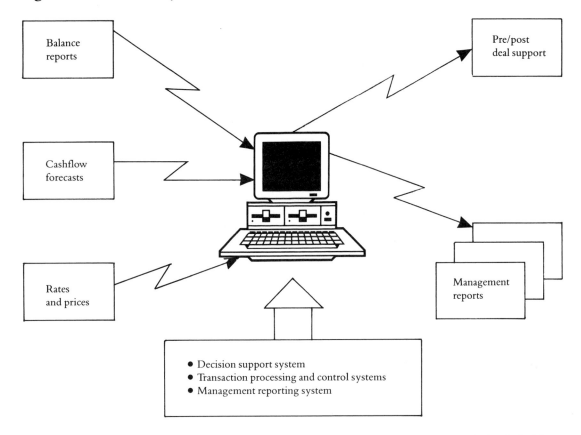

Balance reports from the banks can, in their simplest form, be obtained by telephoning the banks holding the corporate accounts. This procedure is widely used because of its low cost but it involves a relatively high proportion of administrative time. A fully automated treasury workstation could use autodial facilities to gain access to all the cleared bank balance reporting systems, and would feed the information into the workstation.

Cashflow forecast inputs can be simply prepared on spreadsheet facilities, and can be further developed using bureau based arrangements, standard applications or bespoke systems. If a company has its own cashflow forecasting system, a bridge needs to be built between that system and the workstation.

Data on interest and exchange rates are supplied to the workstation via a system like Reuter Monitor or Telerate which gets indication rates from dealing rooms worldwide.

Corporate treasurers can obtain workstation capability by buying a package and building the balance to match their specific requirements or developing a custom-built system.

The primary suppliers of treasury workstation package software fall into two groups. The first group is comprised of the banks which, with a few exceptions, have added components of treasury workstation capability to their electronic banking systems. These modules are usually developed and marketed as part of a product enhancement programme for the electronic banking systems.

The second group of suppliers includes the software houses which have developed treasury workstation software or treasury systems software. This software is often developed initially to meet the specifications of one treasury department, and is subsequently generalised for wider sale.

Selecting a treasury workstation

It is fair to say that any company which sets out to purchase a treasury workstation will have to accept a compromise between its ideal requirement and what is available in the market. This is partly due to the variable requirements of different companies and partly due to the increased development work still to be done to existing systems.

It has been estimated that 50% of the work of a treasury department is standard, while 25% is particular to an industry and another 25% is particular to the individual company. These figures highlight the difficulties which workstation producers face in trying to develop a package to meet the needs of the maximum number of companies.

For a treasurer selecting a workstation, there will be some essential features without which the system will not be worthwhile. It is up to the individual treasurer to decide upon his particular priorities. However, the system must be 'user friendly' and relatively simple to use, otherwise it will be unpopular with treasury staff and the company will not derive maximum benefit from its investment.

Many workstation providers will make small modifications to their systems to suit the needs of individual customers. The company should list all the areas where the system falls short of their ideal requirements and approach the supplier to see if any of these areas can be addressed.

Any company buying a workstation can reasonably expect to be provided with a list of current users of that system. It is also most important that the prospective customer should be able to visit an existing user to see how the system functions in practice. This is bound to highlight areas which have not emerged in the supplier's demonstration. A reputable workstation supplier will arrange a meeting between a prospective and an existing user of their system. This relies upon the goodwill of the system users but in practice most users are quite willing to give the time to discuss their workstation with another treasurer.

Before attending any demonstration of a treasury workstation, the treasurer should make a list of his particular needs so that he can check each one during the course of the demonstration. As a starting point, we have included a requirements checklist as Appendix 5.2. This checklist only represents the main requirements of a typical treasury and, therefore, needs to be amended and expanded before use. In addition to ensuring that the system can cope with his particular treasury department, the treasurer should also consider the following questions:

- What machine does the system run on?
- What are the costs of the hardware and software?
- What are the modelling capabilities?
- What are the accounting and control capabilities?
- Does the system log transactions and provide aggregated reports for management information?
- What are the networking capabilities?
- Does the system have fixed or free format screens?
- What is the number and location of existing installations?
- Does the system link to:

  - Bank reporting systems?
  - Other bank's supplied systems?
  - Interest and exchange rate data?

- What are the planned future developments for the system?

After attending a workstation demonstration, the treasurer should make brief notes about the system and its strengths and weaknesses. This is important as the treasurer is likely to be attending several demonstrations of different systems and the notes will be a useful reminder when he comes to make his final comparisons.

Some treasurers review the existing workstations available in the market and, finding that none of them completely matches their needs, produce a bespoke system tailor made for the particular company. This method can produce a workstation which exactly matches the needs of the company. The disadvantages of this route tend to be:

> Cost: bespoke products are expensive in terms of development costs

> Time: such a system will be slow to reach completion

> Maintenance: systems require constant modification otherwise they become obsolete. A company which produces a bespoke system must be prepared to make a continuous investment of time and money in order to maintain the system.

Bespoke treasury workstations tend to be worthwhile only for large companies with high volumes of treasury transactions. For other companies, it is usually better to select the best of the 'off-the-shelf' workstations. As workstations are being continually developed, they are moving more into line with the needs of the majority of companies.

Difficulties affecting the development of workstations

Three types of problem have affected the development of treasury workstations as an integrated set of treasury systems. These relate to integrating the many inputs to the workstation, linking the workstation to the company's existing systems and networking the systems.

The inputs which have to be integrated into the workstation are the bank balance reporting system, bank electronic funds transfer capability, the company's cashflow forecasting system, and interest and exchange rates provided by outside services.

Linking the treasury workstation into the company's existing systems involves the company's existing cashflow forecasting system as well as its management and financial accounting system. This would allow, for example, the workstation to have direct input from the company's cashflow forecasting systems and to generate output directly into the company's accounting system.

The difficulties of this link are shown in, for example, the way in which the company accounts for a difference in exchange. This will be determined by whether it is a US company following American accounting standards (for example, FASB 52) or a UK company following UK rulings, (for example, SSAP 20), or whether it follows other rulings. It will also be affected by the tax regimes in the country concerned which have different treatments for realised and unrealised losses and gains on foreign exchange. Within one company operating in different countries, a number of different methods may be used for calculating differences in exchange based not only on accounting and tax requirements but also on different product categories or methods of financing.

Networking the different systems presents problems of enabling a treasury workstation in one treasury centre to communicate with another workstation based in a different centre or the same centre.

Regardless of the nature of the company's business or the approaches and attitudes of its treasury department, there are core elements which must be logged and reported for all transactions. A spot transaction, for example, involves the counterparty, the currency sold, the currency purchased, the contract date, and the maturity date. Similar core information is required for forward contracts, placing investments, raising finance, entering into currency or interest swaps or options and other regular transactions.

Differences among treasuries - including types of cashflow associated with the company's products, attitudes to cost or profit centres, and techniques for performance measurement - mean that transactions have to be aggregated in various ways for individual companies. There are also differences in required levels of reporting detail, format and frequency.

The necessity of meeting these differing requirements means that the workstation must bring together the treasury systems of the organisation with enough flexibility in the aggregation of information to enable the treasurer to personalise the system.

The future of treasury workstations

In the development of treasury workstations, the key idea will be integration, encompassing inputs from the banks, company cashflow forecasting systems, company accounting systems, and the suppliers of interest and foreign exchange rates.

In a 1985 survey by Business International of 200 European corporations, 45% of respondents believed that they would become more centralised in their treasury activities over the next three years; 81% said that they would be taking on electronic bank reporting services; 57% thought that their new or existing treasury operations would be primarily electronically based; and 63% felt that they had an increasing need for real-time information services such as Reuter Monitor or Telerate.

With the tendency towards centralisation of treasury functions, there will be an increasing need for electronic treasury workstations which are integrated with bank balance reporting systems and the providers of independent real-time information.

Key action points

In considering the application of a treasury workstation, the following actions should be taken:

- Review the functions of the treasury department - what are the requirements for a treasury workstation?
- Identify products which are available in the market which could possibly meet the treasury's requirements.
- Contact those producers and provide them with the list of requirements or specification produced.
- Attend demonstrations of the individual systems - identify those areas where they do and do not satisfy the requirements.
- Consider the results of the demonstrations - do any of the systems meet requirements to an acceptable level?
- Never be afraid to ask for a second demonstration of a system or to ask questions.
- Ask the supplier to provide a list of current users and to set up a meeting with one such user.
- Ask the supplier to provide a list of current users and to set up a meeting with one such user.

APPENDIX 5.1

How to choose a bank balance reporting system

	Checklist of Requirements	*Typically on offer today*
1	Balances given for current day	Generally yes
2	Balances given for previous day	Generally yes
3	Indication given of value date transactions as separate from cleared transactions	Generally yes
4	What length of balance history is available	From five to 91 days
5	Input from which countries	Varies: Countries with branches of bank - all countries with access to SWIFT
6	How frequently is information updated	Varies: Daily - real-time
7	How far ahead can clearing items be identified	Generally two to five days
8	Can back-up data be shown for items:	
	a By account	Generally yes
	b By transaction	Generally yes
	c By bank charge	Generally no
9	Can funds transmission instructions be sent electronically	Generally yes
10	Can funds be transmitted electronically from other banks	Generally no
11	How far ahead can funds transmission instructions be stored	Varies: Cannot be stored in advance - infinite number of days
12	Can a summary schedule of transactions be indicated by type	Generally yes
13	What access is there to other banks, if not available then there will be the inconvenience of numerous cash management systems	Generally has to be negotiated individually
14	What are the security arrangements	User IDs, passwords, test keys
15	What hardware is used	IBM PC and compatibles.

APPENDIX 5.2

The treasury workstation: requirements checklist

	Requirements	*Comments/Reference*

General

1. Multi-user facility: a number of workstations should be able to access the software simultaneously.

2. Multi-location requirement, ie it should be possible to locate workstations in different offices.

3. Multi-tasking capability. Two or more tasks need to be performed simultaneously.

4. The system must have good access security with secure but unobtrusive procedures.

5. Good data back-up with fast and easy to use procedures.

6. Real-time processing and up-to-date information.

7. Short response time, generally no more than about five seconds, especially for the modelling functions.

8. There must be adequate internal controls

9. Data transfer to and from other systems

10. Automatic update of interest and foreign exchange rates from an external source.

11. Printed output to be available on-line or stored for batch processing when required

Cashflow forecasting

12. Monthly three-month rolling forecast

13. Quarterly 12-month rolling forecast

14. Monthly 12-month review of forecasting performance

Modelling

15. Evaluation of investment and financing alternatives

16. Evaluation of foreign currency hedging options

17. Cash position forecasts by currency

18. Investment, financing and foreign currency hedging plans

19. Funds diary in maturity date order showing committed transactions

Transaction recording

20   Transaction recording, amendment and updating

21   Production of deal slips and confirmation letters

Transaction reporting

22   A list of reports required is given below. However, it is likely that ad-hoc reports, enquiries or new regular reports will be necessary

23   Daily transaction listings by transaction type and by reporting group as specified by user.

       Listings of forward foreign exchange deals and currency options to show estimated profit-and-loss as a result of undertaking these

       User to input estimated spot rates at maturity of individual contracts and not spot deals.

24   Daily cash position summary by currency

25   Daily journal vouchers are required as transactions are executed.

       A monthly summary of all journal vouchers should also be produced including month-end accrual journals

26   Monthly and on request counterparty business analysis report

27   Monthly summary of forward foreign exchange deals and currency options closed during the month. These must be valued against the spot rate on maturity date in order to show opportunity profit-and-loss. This should be compared against the original estimated profit-and-loss

28   Monthly, or as required, summary of all open foreign exchange deals and option contracts. The reports must produce a maturity profile of open contracts valued against the market

29   Monthly investment and financing reports

30   Exception reports listing instances when exception criteria are met. Criteria to be defined by users

31   Monthly key performance measures report. Summary of performance measures for investment, financing and foreign exchange transactions based on all the above reports

CHAPTER 6

The networks and systems

As we have seen in earlier chapters, in the last few years there has been a dramatic increase in the range of electronic banking services available to the treasurer. Underpinning these developments in the provision of electronic banking services are a variety of networks and systems of which the treasurer should be aware. Accordingly, in this chapter we review briefly the main interbank networks (SWIFT, CHAPS and CHIPS) and the bank to user networks that have brought electronic banking into the treasurer's office.

We start by looking at interbank networks, that is networks used to pass information and payments between banks, often on a global basis. We have kept the following descriptions non-technical where possible and where this would not impair a clear understanding of the system involved.

Interbank networks 1 : SWIFT

During the 1950s and 1960s, the growth in international banking business began to exceed the capacity of paper-based manual systems. The need for a fast, safe, computerised system for transferring funds globally grew to paramount importance. Accordingly, in the late 1960s, a group of European and North American banks began a study into systems to satisfy this need that led eventually to the establishment of SWIFT.

The Society for Worldwide Interbank Financial Telecommunication (SWIFT) was established in 1973 by 239 banks in 15 countries as a non-profit, bank-owned, co-operative society.

SWIFT was established to create and operate a specialised data-processing and telecommunication system to process interbank financial transaction instructions between member banks in an automated and highly secure environment. SWIFT does not create or execute banking transactions, these functions are reserved to banks. SWIFT is a service organisation dedicated to meeting a number of specialised service needs relating to interbank financial transactions.

Since inception, SWIFT has experienced a steadily growing volume of transactions among a steadily increasing number of banks on all five continents. The advantages for these banks and their customers are unparalleled speed, accuracy, and security at the lowest possible cost because SWIFT is a non-profit, co-operative society, owned and controlled by the member banks who use SWIFT services.

What swift offers the corporate treasurer

- Essentially SWIFT offers improved international transaction processing in terms of speed, cost and security. The term 'transaction' encompasses most international financial functions such as customer transfers, bank transfers, foreign exchange confirmations, credit/debit confirmations, statements, collections, documentary credits, and interbank securities trading
- It is easier and faster to send a SWIFT message than a telex or letter. This is because the system uses standardised formats, and the procedure for approval and authorisation is shorter and more efficient. Both these steps are performed on the SWIFT terminal and, once authorisation and verification is complete, the message will be sent automatically
- The instructions will also be executed faster at the receiving end as SWIFT can be linked directly to the mainframe of the receiving banks
- SWIFT is cheaper than any other type of message, and the shorter handling time should result

in a lower commission to the bank (although this is not always the case)

- Whilst telex messages can be intercepted and decoded, the electronic coding of SWIFT messages make it impossible to access them while in the system. Even SWIFT staff are unable to read messages passing through the system
- SWIFT is linked with Cedel and Euroclear (Eurobond settlements systems) allowing the rapid clearance and movement of Euro portfolios. SWIFT is also a better distribution system for the prospectus of a new issue than the traditional telex as, by using a simple command, the user can distribute his message worldwide without having to spend time and money on repetitive telexes
- The SWIFT system allows banks to supply corporates with up-to-date cash management information, such as cleared balances.

Figure 6.1 illustrates how a typical corporate would use SWIFT and some of the facilities available.

Figure 6.1: How a typical payment instruction is translated into a SWIFT message

Your company, London Software Ltd, issues a payment instruction for $10,000 to its bank, Barclays Bank in London, to pay for imports from its supplier, Harmoney Inc, in New York. Harmoney Inc is banking with Chase Manhattan Bank NA in New York. This is how your order will be executed on the SWIFT system.

Original instructions	SWIFT execution
Sending bank - Barclays Bank, London	BARCGB2
Type of instruction - customer transfer	100
Destination bank - Chase Manhattan, New York	CHASUS33
Reference number import file 12345	:20: 12345
Value date, currency, amount	:32A: 851231USD10000,
By order	:50: London Software Ltd
Beneficiaries	:59: Harmoney Inc, New York
To bank information	:72: /CABLEBEN/

The last line, field 72, will ensure that the beneficiary will receive a cable advice of the payment from his bank. You can also instruct /PHONEBEN/ or /TELEXBEN/, and your supplier will receive a phone advice or telex advice respectively. Additional fields will allow you to insert his account number, his sorting number (for the United Kingdom) or CHIPS code for banks in the United States.

The above illustration shows a code 100 type of instruction, ie a customer transfer. Other types are as follows:

Group Number	Product
100	Customer transfers
200	Bank transfers
300	Currency operations
400	Collections and services
500	Securities
600	Unassigned
700	Documentary instruments
800	Payment instrument
900	Common group

Ownership, membership and organisation of SWIFT

SWIFT is registered under Belgian law, its headquarters are in Brussels and it is owned by the member banks who use the society's services. Each member bank owns at least one share but share ownership is allocated in proportion to traffic volumes sent on the system.

Board members are elected annually by the whole membership at an annual general meeting. Any member country, or group of countries, accounting for over 1½% of the total system traffic is entitled to nominate one board member, while 6% or more of traffic entitles the members to nominate two board members.

SWIFT distinguishes between two categories of banks - members and users. The headquarters of a bank is both a member and user while a branch or a wholly owned affiliate can only be a user (the traffic of which is allocated to the headquarters). The relationship between SWIFT and its members and user banks is very close and dynamic. Within SWIFT's co-operative structure, member and user banks are simultaneously shareholders and customers for SWIFT services (Figure 6.2).

Figure 6.2: The SWIFT organisation

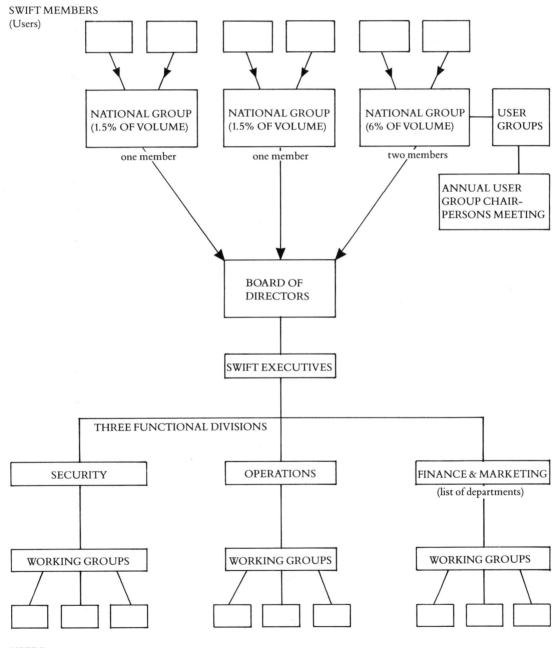

Aside from representation nationally through national SWIFT groups, members and users in each country meet in user groups (representing national members and all users located in that country). The chairmen of user groups meet annually in Brussels to examine operational problems and possible solutions.

SWIFT also organises working groups composed of specialists from a number of member banks in different countries to formulate recommendations concerning standards, new message-types, and potential new service applications. Working groups are usually created by board decision and are provided with very specific instructions upon which to develop a recommendation. Working group recommendations are submitted to the board of directors for consideration.

All members are invited to attend the Annual General Meeting at which the SWIFT budget is submitted for approval, board members are elected, and a number of other policy matters are submitted to the shareholders.

Objectives of SWIFT

When SWIFT was created, six primary objectives were defined for the company. The system should be:

- Available. The SWIFT system is available to member and user banks 24 hours a day, seven days a week
- Rapid. Bank-to-bank information is transmitted worldwide in a matter of seconds
- Standardised. Transaction instructions are entered into the system in standardised data format permitting automated handling while eliminating language interpretation problems
- Auditable. Detailed transaction records and identification ensure clear audit reports
- Controllable. Control procedures provide member banks with several levels of input, audit and verification coupled with effective sequence controls and delivery status reports
- Secure. SWIFT assumes financial liability for the completeness, accuracy and confidentiality of transaction instructions from and to the point of connection to member banks' circuits.

The SWIFT system

The technological infrastructure of the SWIFT system consists of the original system (called SWIFT I) and the new system that will progressively replace it (called SWIFT II). The new system is a modular design that will allow SWIFT to be easily expanded to meet new geographical demands and to handle higher volumes of transactions.

SWIFT I (Figure 6.3) is structured as a relatively simple computerised system designed to 'store and forward' interbank transaction instructions. The characteristics of SWIFT I are a centralised structure focused on three manned Operating Centres (OPCs) located in Belgium, Holland, and the United States. These OPCs receive, validate, store, process, and deliver all interbank transaction instructions moving on the system.

Operating Centres are connected to Regional Processors (RPCs) located in each member country or region. RPCs are unmanned computer installations. Member banks connect to SWIFT through the RPC serving their geographic location, and the RPCs are in turn connected to one of the OPCs. Regional Processors serve as the input and output gateways for transactions moving on the system and handle the various format and line protocols required as well as providing the first point of transaction concentration.

SWIFT II (Figure 6.3), began phasing into operation in 1985 and should fully replace SWIFT I some time in 1987. This is a relatively more complex system designed around a 'transaction processing' concept and using a decentralised approach based on more distributed processing and modular expansion.

The characteristic structure of SWIFT II calls for at least two System Control Centres (SCCs) manned by permanent staff. System Control Centres will perform overall control and monitoring functions for the system, provide archival functions and provide direct support and interface support to member banks.

In SWIFT II, transaction processing will take place in so-called slice processors. Any number of these can be located wherever necessary or convenient. They are unmanned installations and will handle the message processing functions centralised at the OPCs in the SWIFT I structure. Their functions include validation, queue, and storage of incoming transactions prior to initiative delivery through the system.

Figure 6.3: The technological infrastructure

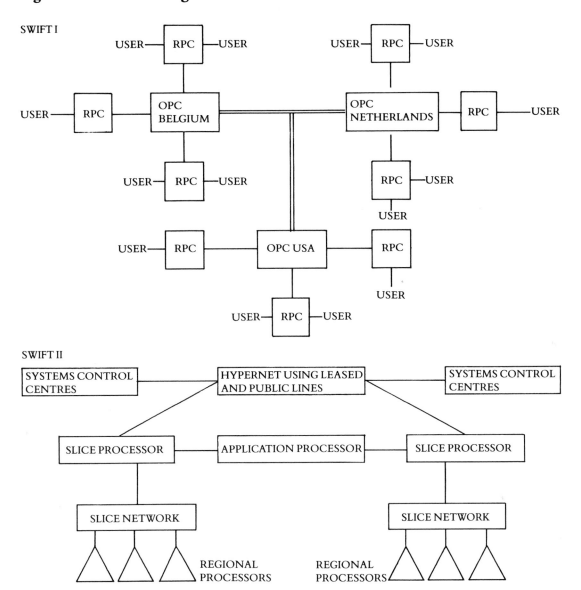

The difference between SWIFT I and II can be illustrated by considering the path of a message from New Zealand to Australia. Whereas with SWIFT I the message would go via the OPC in USA, with SWIFT II the message switching would be performed by a slice processor location in or nearer to Australia - NZ region.

The function of the existing Regional Processors will remain essentially unchanged, but in SWIFT II they can also act as the first point of short-term storage.

SWIFT II will be interconnected through two levels of network (SCC - SLICE, and SLICE - RP) using leased lines (cable, microwave, or satellite) and public networks (telephone, public data networks).

The SWIFT terminal interfaces

The terminal interfaces are simply the hardware used by the user banks and, although they belong to the user banks, they must be tested and approved by SWIFT. They include mainly three types of terminals:

ST100 - Low-cost, stand-alone terminal suitable for a branch or as a back-up. They will not be linked to SWIFT II and therefore will gradually disappear

ST200 - Announced in 1982, this is a multi-terminal system with a batch and mainframe capability designed for the multi-department bank or branch

ST500 - High-speed gateway system to serve between SWIFT and the bank's mainframe.

It is anticipated that the ST200 and ST500 will gradually be replaced by the ST400, a terminal specifically designed for the SWIFT II system.

SWIFT I

Since its inception in 1973, SWIFT has achieved an annual compound growth of 60% in terms of volume of transactions. All major money centres and most major countries, other than some in East Europe and the Middle East, are now covered totalling some 60 countries in all.

The growth in terms of bank and country members and in terms of daily traffic volume is given in Figure 6.4.

Figure 6.4: The first 12 years

(1) GROWTH IN TERMS OF BANK MEMBERS AND COUNTRY MEMBERS

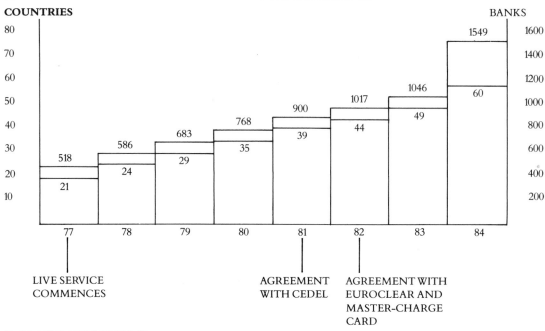

(2) DAILY TRAFFIC VOLUME
DESPITE THE SHARP GROWTH IN NUMBER OF USERS, LEVEL OF DAILY USAGE IS
EXPECTED TO LEVEL OFF, AS 80% OF THE VOLUME IS GENERATED BY ONLY 300 BANKS

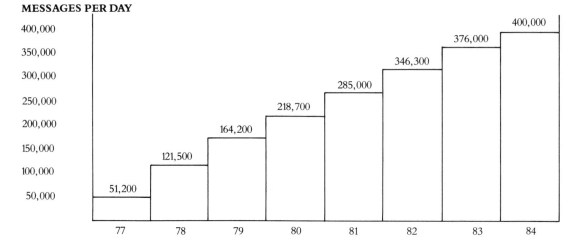

SWIFT II and the future

With SWIFT growing as fast as it has been, it is easy to imagine a single worldwide funds and information transfer system linking all the banks, brokers, corporates (and maybe individuals) through an on-line, simple to use computer network. However, in reality, this is some way off and there are a number of problems to be overcome:

- The big money centre banks (who are also the big shareholders of SWIFT) have invested huge sums of money in creating their own systems and networks and are increasingly using them as fee generators and as marketing tools against their rivals. It is unlikely that they would refrain from competing with SWIFT
- By linking the corporate directly to the SWIFT system the treasurer would be able not only to have direct information links to 1,500 banks in the world but also to issue transactions directly. The role of the banks would be reduced to 'data brokers' - suppliers of balances and rates. Banks would also lose balances as a result because no excess funds would be left overnight.

Despite this, it seems likely that SWIFT will be the major funds and information tool of the future. What is more interesting, is to speculate on the intermediary stages before we reach this target, this could include the following:

- Banks including SWIFT in their systems. For example, a Citibank client who is using Citibank electronic banking issues a letter of credit in his office in London to be opened in Citibank, Hong Kong. Citibank uses its own network to transfer the letter of credit to the London branch office but uses SWIFT message group type 700 to transmit the letter of credit to Citibank, Hong Kong, and once there, again uses its own network to deliver the message to the supplier
- Customised SWIFT systems. SWIFT has the capability to develop tailor-made systems to be used by individual banks as their own electronic banking products. Bank clients could use SWIFT formats but would still have to operate through their banks. This arrangement could also be on a group basis (that is groups of banks agreeing to use a common SWIFT system)
- SWIFT could become a private company owned by some banks and operating on a profit basis. Thus, the banks will maintain their return on investments and competitiveness.

Interbank networks 2: CHAPS

In Volume 1 Chapter 3, we looked at cash transmission techniques available to the corporate treasurer. As stated, one of the more recent techniques is the Clearing House Automated Payments System, commonly known as CHAPS, which began operation in February 1984. In summary, this payment method offers the corporate treasurer the same day guaranteed settlement of transactions over £10,000 anywhere in the United Kingdom.

In this chapter, we look at how such payments are processed in practice and at the underlying systems and networks.

How a CHAPS payment is processed

As stated, CHAPS will only handle payments over £10,000, thereby restricting its potential use for private individuals. Nevertheless, let us take as an example a transaction that is likely to be very familiar, namely house purchase. In such a situation, CHAPS would be used as follows (Figure 6.5).

Funds deposited with the buyer's solicitor, and held in the solicitor's bank branch account must be transferred to the account of the seller's solicitor before contracts are exchanged.

On the day of completion therefore, details of the payment are keyed into a computer terminal in the clearing bank branch using the 'CHAPS format', an agreed form of payment message.

The message is transmitted over the telephone lines to the clearing bank's computer centre where it is authorised, authenticated and passed to the CHAPS 'gateway'.

This is essentially a powerful minicomputer running the special programs necessary to prepare the

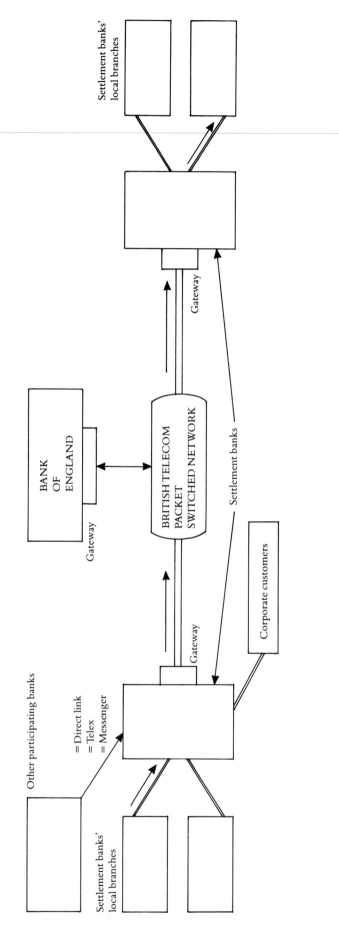

Figure 6.5: The CHAPS system

70

message for transmission over British Telecom's Packet Switched Service (PSS), a new and efficient data communications network which will be the basis of most of the United Kingdom's electronic funds transfer systems in future.

The message moves to the gateway owned by the recipient clearer by the fastest and most economical route. It is then passed to the bank's main computers for accounting purposes and switched through to the branch holding the account of the seller's solicitor. The message is coded and carries its own authentication. An acknowledgement that the message has been received safely passes back across the PSS from the receiving gateway to the transmitting gateway.

So, in seconds a payment has been made that by traditional methods would take hours and involve a ritual of telex and telephone messages, not to mention messengers walking from bank to bank through the City clutching written payment instructions.

The CHAPS system

The technology of CHAPS is reasonably advanced. Its core is a communications network between the clearing banks using British Telecom's Packet Switching Services (PSS). The PSS is the first purpose-built public data transmission network in the United Kingdom and achieves the highest levels of operational efficiency and security.

The clearing banks and the Bank of England jointly referred to as Settlement Banks, are linked into the PSS Tandem computers which, with software common to all the banks, provide the communications, routing and audit functions which ensure that the system operates in a secure environment. Each 'gateway' also contains bank specific software which enables the bank systems to be connected to the central switching system.

Recognising the immense value of the payments which pass through CHAPS, the security of the system has been a paramount factor in its design. Each payment is individually identified by time stamping and sequential numbering. Full message authentication and encryption is applied. This means that every payment is coded as it passes between banks making almost impossible any unauthorised attempts to interfere. Full contingency procedures have been established for extreme conditions or failure at any point in the system.

The development and administration of CHAPS is co-ordinated by the Committee of London Clearing Bankers which has established the regulations for operating the system. CHAPS operates between 9.30 am and 3 pm although this, together with the minimum amount for each payment of £10,000, is reviewed regularly. At the close of each day, settlement between each bank and the Bank of England automatically follows 'cut-off' at 3 pm.

The significance of the CHAPS systems design for the corporate treasurer

Firstly, any bank customer who wishes to make an immediate money transfer has a choice as indicated in Figure 6.5 of the way in which he accesses CHAPS. Instructions can be passed to the account holding branch which will then initiate a CHAPS payment instead of using the telephonic transfer system. If the beneficiary has to be advised of the receipt of funds, a mandatory advice can be included in the payment message and the payee bank will make every effort to ensure that their customer is advised. As far as corporate treasurers are concerned, transfer instructions will be passed to an account holding branch in the usual way. The only change is that the payments will be transmitted much more rapidly.

As an alternative however, and this is where CHAPS really is so revolutionary, a direct electronic connection can be established which will enable a treasurer to initiate payments from his own office and, similarly, to be advised of incoming transfers. With a computer terminal in his own office, the speed of such payments and advice of receipts will be measured in seconds and because there is no manual intervention, there are obvious implications for both efficiency and cost.

It is because of the ability to access CHAPS directly that such an opportunity is presented to the corporate treasurer. Clearly, the ability to monitor incoming funds as they are received and to dictate precisely the timing of outward payments, significantly enhances the management of cashflow and bank balances. The system is available throughout the United Kingdom and will clearly have an impact in making the need for a City presence less critical.

CHAPS breaks the geographic confines of the town clearing. This latter factor may well become an important influence in its effect upon rationalisation and relocation decisions. Because CHAPS leads to reduced reliance on cheques for funds transfer, the forecasting of outward cashflows is considerably more precise. There is less reliance upon the guesstimates which are currently necessary to cope with the variable and unpredictable delays in the timings of the presentations of cheques.

For efficient treasurers, CHAPS provides the opportunity to settle the larger trade payments on a known date, having negotiated with the supplier the date on which cleared value would have been received had the payments been made by cheque. Thus certainty and precision are provided in cashflow forecasting for both the buying and the supplying companies.

The clearing banks have been criticised for not providing a standard terminal with which to access the CHAPS system. It is interesting to note that when the banks provide common systems they are accused of operating as a cartel. In the case of CHAPS, each clearing bank is competing to provide the most effective terminal package. The specification and capability of what each bank provides differ quite significantly with each bank believing that it has provided the most attractive combination of services for its potential CHAPS customers. Ultimately this must be advantageous for the banks' customers as each bank is keen to promote the product which it regards as being superior in level of service and price.

Clearly, CHAPS provides a significant contribution to electronic banking and is becoming a cornerstone for sterling cash management and funds transfer. It is already under evaluation for inclusion as the funds transfer mechanism for other major electronic developments.

Interbank networks 3: CHIPS

While CHAPS went live in early 1984, its New York equivalent, CHIPS (Clearing House Interbank Payments System), was established as long ago as 1970. Although CHAPS is much more 'state of the art' in terms of technology, the same principles underpin both CHAPS and CHIPS. The operation of CHIPS is described below.

CHIPS is responsible for an estimated 90% of all international interbank dollar transfers. Daily dollar volume is currently around $300 billion, involving around 100,000 transactions with peaks at much higher figures.

The New York Clearing House Association, which set up CHIPS, comprises 12 major New York banks and was originally formed for the clearance of cheques. CHIPS was established in 1970 replacing the cumbersome clearing system as it became essential to speed and simplify the processing of the ever-increasing number of interbank transfers in the New York area. Initially, it was restricted to international payments, but within a short time interbank transfers were brought into the system. The CHIPS participants are 22 'settling' banks (the 12 New York clearing banks, nine Edge Act corporations [banks dealing purely in foreign exchange, trade finance and any other non-domestic transaction] and one other New York commercial bank) together with other institutions which include Edge Act units of US banks outside New York and branches and agencies of foreign banks, making a total of around 100. The 'settling' participants are simply those who settle for themselves or through whom other participants must settle.

CHIPS is a computerised telecommunications payment system. Each paying participant transmits payment messages through electronic terminals to a central computer maintained by the clearing house which then records and transmits to the receiving participant. At the end of the business day, the computer provides information advising each participant of its net position.

Credit exposure

Prior to October 1 1981, all these payments were in clearing house funds or next day funds. Final settlement was not effected until the following business day through transfers from net debtors to net creditors using the Federal Reserve Bank wire transfer system. Settling participants would settle their own positions, and those of the other non-settling participants in Federal funds through their accounts at the Federal Reserve Bank.

In theory, if a settling participant decided for any reason not to cover a participant's debt position, all transactions to and from that participant through CHIPS would have been reversed and a new attempt made to settle. The unwinding would have returned the failed participant to its original position but could have created havoc with the positions of the other participants who expected funds. All payments were irrevocable, but conditional on final settlement the following business day.

The Clearing House and the Federal Reserve had been trying for many years to reduce this overnight credit exposure and the Herstatt experience in 1974 may have provided a much needed stimulus. By collapsing in 'mid-settlement' in the gap between receipt of Deutschemarks and payment of dollar funds, the Herstatt Bank illustrated the dangers of delayed settlements of funds.

Finally, a new system for same-day settlement was developed and implemented bringing it into line with practices in other countries. Under this system it is no longer necessary to delay settlement until the next business day. As of October 1 1981, CHIPS payments were settled at the end of each business day in same-day funds through transfers at the Federal Reserve Bank.

There is no longer overnight uncertainty on whether participants will be able to settle for their payments. It does not eliminate the risk but reduces it to an intraday position and limits any possible unwinding to one day's transactions instead of two. Payments are still irrevocable, but not final until settlement has been agreed by 5.30 pm US Eastern Standard Time.

The Federal Reserve Bank has agreed to assist the Clearing House by providing a special CHIPS settlement account in its books. Settlement is then made by any participant according to predetermined settlement agreements. The Federal Reserve Bank has determined that any participant who has an account at the New York Fed can settle its own position, if it chooses to do so. With same-day settlement on each business day, every settling participant that has a debit position settles by making a payment to the special CHIPS account at the New York Fed by 5.45 pm. Once all debtor settling participants have transferred funds into the settlement account, the New York Clearing House releases the funds to the creditor settling participants' accounts at the New York Fed before 6 pm. The net balance of the settlement account is then nil.

There are no plans at present to expand CHIPS into currencies other than dollars and limitations in its present charter prelude the clearing house from geographic expansion beyond New York City.

Bank to user networks

Having examined the main interbank networks, let us now look briefly at the bank to user networks that support the supply of electronic banking services.

Some of these networks make use of British Telecom's Packet Switched Service while some use dedicated computer facilities. Most common however is the use of time-sharing bureaux such as GEISCO and ADP. These bureaux connect subscribers to a suite of powerful central computers that hold individual programs for each set of subscribers. The best known network is that run by General Electric through its subsidiary GEISCO. A call to a local number enables a terminal to be connected through a modem to GEISCO's system, which includes 450 computers which connect more than 26 countries. Over 6,000 users can access the network at the same time and the application of message switching technology is such that large users can be given the impression that the whole network has been dedicated to them on a continuous basis.

Some banks have purchased or set up their own dedicated networks (Chase Manhattan with IDC and CDN, Manufacturers Hanover with Geonet, Citibank with Global Transaction Network (GTN) and Bank of America with B of A Net). This step invariably requires substantial investment and has so far only been taken by the large US banks. With the development of sophisticated independent international networks, for example, SWIFT, investment in dedicated networks is looking increasingly less attractive.

Typical electronic bank to user links

The particular network used to supply electronic banking services is of little concern and largely transparent to the user. This is illustrated by examining a typical electronic bank to user link, the Midland Bank EFT system which uses the ADP time-sharing network. The system configuration is shown in Figure 6.6.

Figure 6.6: Midland bank's corporate EFT system

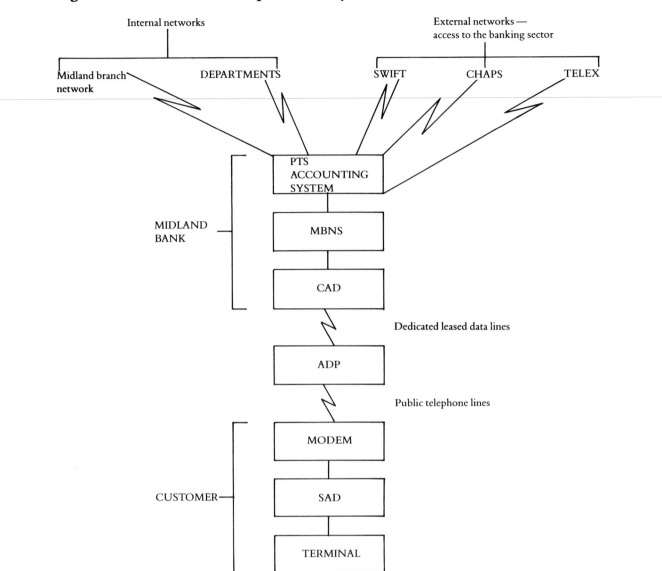

Note: For higher volume users, alternative structures could apply with connection established via leased lines or the Packet Switched Service and using mainframe, micro or minicomputer processing power.

Midland has used ADP to offer customers an electronic link into their own Midland Bank Network System (MBNS) and Payment Transmission System (PTS), which in turn links into SWIFT, CHAPS, Telex and the branch network and departments. The alternative to this electronic link is for customers to pass instructions by telephone and/or in writing to their local Midland branch which will then enter the message into PTS.

To use this system the customer merely has to have installed on his premises a dumb terminal or microcomputer capable of communicating a modem/acoustic coupler and for payments an additional security device known as Satellite Authentication Device (SAD).

To transmit payments, the user dials into the local ADP centre and, once connected, follows the procedure for inputting a payment message. The SAD authenticates the message before it is sent down public telephone lines to ADP and from there to Midland on dedicated leased lines. At Midland Bank, the message is checked by the Central Authentication Device (CAD) before passing into the MBNS and PTS for transfer to the recipient's banks accounts.

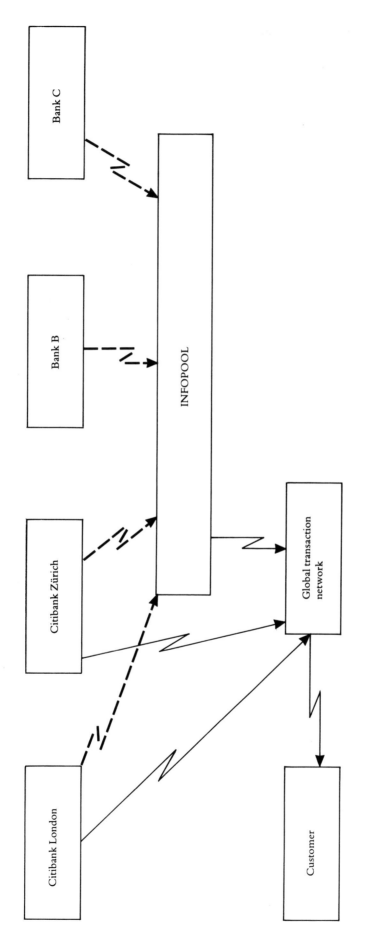

Figure 6.7: Citibank's infopool

ADP's function is to act as a transaction handling centre. ADP hold a suite of application programs and customer files that will check customer log-ons (passwords, terminal authentication), can store a library of regular messages for each customer and store messages until ready for transmission to Midland. Therefore, they offer to Midland Bank a fully functioning communication centre with dedicated computers, a host of telephone lines and specialist staff. This provides the same high level of service to corporates and private users that is available between banks.

Citibank has developed a data pool called Infopool which is based on a mainframe computer in Brussels (Figure 6.7). Customers ask Citibank branches and other banks at which they hold accounts to provide balance and transactions details to Infopool via SWIFT 940 message statements or telex. Infopool can then, on demand, distribute the information through its Global Transaction Network. Infopool provides cleared balances, transaction details and forward clearings as at the close of business the previous day. As well as offering realtime access directly to separate branch computers, Citibank also offers the facility for obtaining consolidated information from its branches and from other banks.

Chemical Bank's Chemlink is similar feeding into GEISCO's Data Exchange. More than 100 banks worldwide provide balances and transaction details to Data Exchange; these are then delivered in a collated form to customers' mainframe or microcomputers.

Key action points

In considering the use of bank systems with a view to their use, the treasurer must decide:

- How the information is required?
- What level of detail is required?
- Which information is required?
- How often is this information required?

The treasurer must ensure that:

- The company can retain flexibility in bank relations.
- The system enables the company to access non-vendor bank account balances.
- Balances incorporate current day credit clearing.
- The funds transfer services have adequate control facilities.
- The system is as simple as possible to operate.

CHAPTER 7

Security and controls

Earlier chapters of this volume have highlighted the increasing sophistication of the treasury function in terms of both organisation and automation. This chapter concentrates on the controls which should be applied to the treasury in order to provide satisfactory levels of security. To manage any organisation or department effectively, management must introduce routines for processing and recording transactions and for generating information which are used for assessing the unit's past performance and future needs. Such routines are commonly referred to as 'systems' and may include both manual and computerised tasks.

Management must also ensure that these systems are operating effectively and they should therefore impose 'internal control procedures' upon them. The nature of these procedures varies considerably from one organisation to another, according to the size, nature, and complexity of the business but they all have the same purpose - to enable management to carry on the business in an orderly manner, safeguard its assets, and ensure, as far as possible, the accuracy and reliability of its records.

As a treasury department deals with the most liquid of assets, cash, and is in the very volatile environment of fluctuating foreign exchange and interest rates, adequate internal controls are of paramount importance.

In this chapter we will firstly look at internal controls in general, define the different types of controls, relate these controls to the treasury department and then examine possible controls over the area of highest risk namely electronic funds transfer.

There are no generally accepted terms to identify the various categories of internal controls. Within this chapter the following categories have however been used:

- Organisational controls
- Procedural controls
- Information systems controls
- EDP controls.

Organisational controls

Organisational structure is a result of management's assignment of responsibility and delegation of authority. The structure defines the functions of individuals responsible for making decisions and establishing policies; it also stipulates the limitations on their authority. Clearly defined responsibilities and limits of authority contribute to a strong control environment.

Such a definition of responsibilities should include:

- How major areas of activity (such as, accounting, tax or treasury) are planned, operated, co-ordinated, and controlled
- Where management policy decisions are taken
- How these policies are communicated to line management.

They should also ensure that major decisions are made by managers who are in a position to assess their overall implications, that staff report to an appropriate level of management and that delegated authority is adequate, appropriate and not excessive.

This definition should normally be recorded on an organisation chart indicating the duties and responsibilities assigned to the various members of staff. Such a definition should also be accompanied by a statement of management policies and objectives. The policies are the base rules by which a treasury should operate to achieve its objectives.

An aspect of organisational control which is particulary important is the segregation of duties, both between individuals and between departments. The underlying principle is that no one person should be in a position to control sufficient stages of processing a transaction so that errors or defalcations could occur without others becoming aware. Ideally the flow of activity should be designed so that the work of one person is either independent of, or serves as a check on, the work of another person. For example, it will usually be desirable to separate the responsibilities for:

- Initiating transactions (for example, foreign exchange dealing)
- Recording transactions (for example, back-office)
- Monitoring activity (for example, reviewing performance reports).

In practice, the operation of this principle of segregation of duties will be influenced by such considerations as the number and experience of the staff available, the volume, complexity and financial significance of the transactions and the costs of maintaining the control.

There is a danger here of assuming that a system of segregation of duties which appears adequate in theory will necessarily function effectively in practice. It is normally not possible to design a system which is proof against fraudulent collusion, especially on the part of those in positions of authority or trust. Equally, a system may be undermined if employees who become aware of irregularities decide not to report them, perhaps because those responsible are either personal friends or senior officials.

Procedural controls

Procedural controls fall into two main categories:

- Documentation flow procedures which are the control procedures built into the system of processing documentation so that one aspect of the system is proved by a subsequent step. A simple example is where an official approves a telex payment instruction on the basis of relevant supporting documentation including evidence that the goods or services were received and that they were ordered by an authorised employee
- Independent control procedures which are superimposed by management but which are independent of the documentation flow system. An example would be the periodic agreement of the settlement clerk's position book with the dealer's dealing pad.

The control imposed by an effective internal and/or external audit department can also be considered procedural in nature.

In times of stress or understaffing it is the independent control procedures which tend to lapse first as the main effort is directed at maintaining the document flow. The failure to carry out these control procedures can undermine the effectiveness of the whole recording system.

Information systems controls

Information systems controls represent those arrangements by which information is produced and supplied to management so that it can be monitored, reviewed, and acted upon.

Some of the major characteristics of a good information system are:

- The information should deal with only the key areas of activity
- The source of information should be clear and it should be possible to obtain more detailed information if necessary

- The information should be available to the appropriate level of management on a timely basis so that it can be used in planning the organisation's day-to-day business affairs
- The information should be easy to understand
- Comparisons with budget and (if useful) with previous periods should be included.

The following are symptoms of an inadequate information system:

- Decisions are often made based on guesses
- There is no effective planning control
- The information is provided in a confused manner and badly explained
- The information is not related to the responsibilities of the managers to whom it is sent
- Insufficient consideration is given to conditions prevailing outside the enterprise
- There are frequent management surprises such as large open positions and large budget variances.

The relative importance of the management information system within an organisation or department will depend on the size of the unit and the values handled. Small units can normally operate effectively with an information system based on personal contact or individual involvement with the other areas of management but larger units need more sophisticated management information to provide assurance that activities are conducted as authorised and to obtain information about the unit's activities and financial position.

To provide this information, a system will be needed that records all activity, both actual deals and discarded quotations, and then produces the necessary reports from this database. Typically, a monthly management reporting package should include reports summarising activity for the month and the month end position, measuring performance and highlighting possible problems that may require management action.

Summaries of activity, for example, the number of deals in a month, can indicate the level of utilisation of resources or even unauthorised activity, say if there are unusually high volumes of transactions. For example, in one instance investigation of unusually high activity in the foreign exchange market led to the dismissal of the treasurer. It transpired that having made a large currency loss on one deal, the treasurer started to 'play the market' in order to recoup his losses. As speculative dealing was against company policy, there was no option but to dismiss the treasurer.

Reports of the month end position, for example, investment balances and funding profiles, give a vital overview of the assets and liabilities under control and can highlight areas for further investigation. For example, should we be borrowing short when interest rates are expected to rise or should we have such a high level of dollar investments when the dollar is likely to fall?

Performance measurement of activity is an area that has been particularly neglected in the context of treasury departments. If properly produced and sensibly interpreted, performance measures can greatly enhance control over a treasury department. By reporting repeatedly poor performances in one area, say currency exposure hedging, a performance measure can highlight a problem, say the need for more or better quality staff, far more powerfully than any number of verbal representations. Equally some measures, for example, average level of idle balances, can indicate external problems, for example, poor cashflow forecasts from the operating departments. Even a single measure, such as average return on investments, can be very revealing. For example, in one instance a fund manager was dismissed after repeatedly producing a return on investment of below that available on government stocks. This had resulted from unwise forays into foreign currency investments.

Another way of highlighting possible problems is exception reporting, whereby a report is produced when exception criteria are met, say when authority limits are breached. The purpose of these reports is to highlight only unusual situations and thereby minimise the volume of management information. Other reports, such as cash position forecasts, can also warn management of the need for possible future action, for example action to meet a forecast cash deficit in excess of established borrowing facilities.

Electronic Data Processing (EDP) controls

Although the objectives and principles of internal control are the same, there are some significant differences between the controls in EDP and non-EDP systems. These differences include the following:

- In EDP systems, certain control procedures leave no documentary evidence of performance (that is, loss of visible management/audit trail). For some other procedures, the evidence of performance is indirect; it may be included in the program logic or in the operator's instructions
- Accounting procedures are often performed by computer programs with information generated automatically based on data previously entered, without further human instructions. There may or may not be visible evidence (that is, audit trail) of these processing steps
- Errors which might be observed in non-EDP systems may go undetected because of the reduced human involvement in computerised processing. There is a danger that errors in processing may be applied to a large number of transactions without being noticed
- With proper controls, EDP systems can provide better reliability than non-EDP systems. This is because EDP systems subject all data to the same procedures and controls. Non-EDP systems are subject to human error on a random basis. However, while computer processing will usually be consistent, errors may still occur, for example, if the computer is incorrectly programmed
- EDP systems may also provide improved controls by subjecting data to control checks which would require an inordinate amount of time to perform manually.

The implementation of adequate EDP controls on a treasury department is made considerably more difficult by the trend towards the use of microcomputers. In a small microcomputer environment some of the following control problems may be found:

- Lack of segregation of duties. Large computer installations usually have separate groups of staff within the EDP department for programming, operations and control of data. In a small computer installation, one or two persons often perform the functions of systems analysis, system design, programming, maintenance of software, and operations. They may also be responsible for controlling data files and entering transactions
- Inadequate software processing controls. Small computer application systems are often purchased from manufacturers or software vendors who may not offer desirable on-line control techniques. Vendors and users may believe that the expense of developing adequate controls and the additional processing costs are not warranted
- Ready access to data files and programs. In many small computer installations, current versions of master files and programs are always available for on-line enquiries and updating, often through the medium of standard utility programs which may be used readily by user staff thus bypassing the specified programmed controls for an application
- Inadequate control over program changes resulting from either the use of easy-to-learn programming languages (for example, BASIC) or of standard utilities
- Inadequate file and program back-up procedures. Many companies which use small computers have all operating and administrative functions located in a single building with no off-site storage facilities readily available. A fireproof safe or filing cabinet may be considered an unnecessary expense. User personnel may not create back-up files because they do not understand the need for them or because of the length of time sometimes necessary to create copy files.

In addition to controls normally found in a manual system, the following controls should generally be installed in an EDP environment:

- Controls conducive to reliable data processing
  — Segregation of duties between EDP function and users and within EDP function
  — Access security (physical and software) to prevent unauthorised changes to input data, data files and computer programs
  — Day-to-day controls over changes to computer programs (such as system software and application programs) and data files
  — Controls over computer operations (to ensure use of correct data files and computer programs only)
- Application systems development controls
  — Development, testing, documentation and implementation of in-house systems
  — Acquisition, testing, approval, documentation and implementation of external accounting packages
- Controls conducive to continuous data processing
  — Physical access restrictions (to prevent destruction or theft of data programs or equipment)

     — Disaster prevention and recovery procedures (for example, back-up of computer facility, data files, computer programs, documentation and key personnel)
- Input controls
     — Controls over user data within the data processing department
     — Key transcription controls (such as the conversion of input into machine readable format, otherwise known as data preparation and data conversion)
- Processing controls
     — Controls over entry of data into on-line systems (for example, authorisation or totalling)
     — Data editing and validation
     — Data processing controls over rejected and suspense transactions
     — Controls to balance the application and master files
     — Reconciliation of output control totals and processing controls with input control totals
     — Reporting of management/audit trails for all significant processing stages.

As can be seen, internal controls are not just security in terms of preventing fraud but are those management checks that ensure a properly functioning and effective organisation.

Treasury department controls

As stated earlier, the treasury department is a high risk area and arguably the highest risk department in any company. For example, a treasury dealer is authorised to commit the company by telephone to relatively large transactions with a counterparty (usually a bank); such authority is normally only afforded to the most senior management. The risks associated with treasury transactions are illustrated in Figure 7.1.

Figure 7.1: Risks associated with treasury transactions

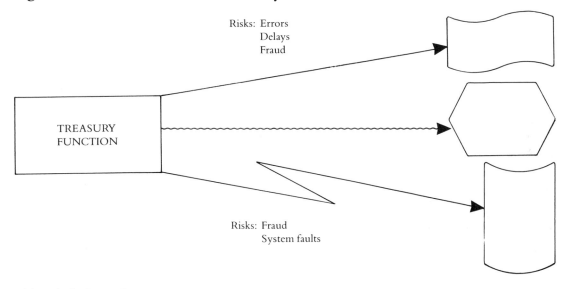

Although the level of risk will depend upon the functions performed and value of transactions handled, in a typical treasury lack of control can result in large cash losses due to:

- Unauthorised or incorrect cash transfer (for example, there is the case of $50 million being transferred to XYZ bank in Paris instead of ABC bank in New York)
- Misappropriated or misplaced cash receipts
- Lack of action to hedge unfavourable foreign exchange or interest rate movements

or can result in lost opportunities due to:

- Inability to take advantage of favourable movements in rates
- Lack of planning and advance warning of, for example, cash surpluses or currency positions
- Inability to delay payments or to choose the most cost effective payments and receipts methods.

Therefore, adequate internal controls need to be installed when establishing a new treasury department or when reviewing and reorganising an existing one. The procedure for implementation and review of internal controls is examined below. The area of Electronic Funds Transfer is separately examined as it is not only a particularly risky area, but may be a discrete addition to the treasury department.

Implementing or reviewing internal controls

In implementing internal controls in a new treasury department or when reviewing existing controls, the first step must be to understand clearly each area of risk. In order to do this, the treasury operation should be systematically analysed, for example in the following categories:

- Cash management
- Use of banking services
- Funds management
- Currency management
- Interest rate exposure management
- Foreign exchange rate exposure management
- Information needs and reporting.

Accordingly, we have included in Appendix 7.1 a framework for understanding and evaluating the relative importance of each area of risk. Only when the relative importance of each area is known can sensible and appropriate levels of control be instituted.

Once a clear understanding of each treasury function has been obtained, the controls needed in each area can be determined. Accordingly, we have set out in Appendix 7.2 examples of questions that should be included in a checklist when reviewing existing controls. Equally, if implementing new controls, such a checklist would indicate what controls are needed and what they must achieve.

Electronic funds transfer

As we have said, the treasury is arguably the highest risk department in an organisation. Within the treasury department, arguably the highest risk area is Electronic Funds Transfer (EFT).

For a treasurer the methods available for EFT which are of concern to us are generally based on a terminal in his office linked by a network to his bank. The terminal can be a microcomputer on which he can also perform other treasury functions, or it can be a dumb terminal dedicated solely to EFT. The network can be over leased or public lines and could link the treasurer not only to his bank, but also to an EFT network such as CHAPS.

Clearly then, there are three areas of risk in an EFT system:

- The user end
- The network
- The bank end.

From a treasurer's viewpoint, the latter two areas are largely outside his control, therefore when looking at EFT systems he must ensure that there are adequate built-in controls.

At the 'user end' while the treasurer has considerably more control, he can only really enhance and strengthen built-in controls. It is virtually impossible to compensate satisfactorily for a lack of built-in controls. Effective built-in controls have the added benefit of prompting well-controlled user procedures, for example, segregation of duties will be enhanced by a hierarchical password system that prevents one person both inputting and authorising a payment.

A comprehensive list of the built-in controls to look for in an EFT system is given in Appendix 7.3. The full list can be summarised into the following types of controls:

- Logical (programmed) access controls which allow only authorised users to access the system and only up to their authorised limit

- Authorisation and other controls to ensure only bona fide messages are transmitted
- Transaction recording controls to ensure a full record of all activity.

Key action points

To summarise, when reviewing or implementing new internal controls the following key action points should be noted:

- Evaluate the relative level of risk for the company in each treasury area.
- Do the existing internal controls and controls built into EFT and computerised systems offer adequate protection against the risks?
- Consider methods of improving controls to reach an acceptable level of security.
- Present a cost/risk analysis to management to underline the need for a control budget.
- When evaluating new computerised systems look for those with good built-in, programmed controls.
- During the implementation of controls, allow a period for training of staff, testing and amendment.

APPENDIX 7.1

A risk analysis framework

	BACKGROUND INFORMATION CHECKLIST		
1	**Summary**		
	Based on the information collected on the attached schedule and as suggested below, are the following areas significant to the business?		
		Yes	No
	Cash management — working capital controls — cash mobilisation	☐	☐
	Use of banking services	☐	☐
	Funds management	☐	☐
	Interest rate exposure	☐	☐
	Exchange exposure	☐	☐
	Currency management	☐	☐
	Information needs and reporting	☐	☐

2	General
2.1	General nature of the business
	— Main products and geographical markets
	— Level of diversification
	— Level of vertical integration
	— Cyclical nature of activities
	— Number of major subsidiaries/divisions
	— Size of workforce
2.2	How centralised are the organisation's activities in terms of the:
	— Purchasing function
	— Production function
	— Selling function
	— Distribution function
	— Accounting function
	— Treasury function
2.3	Define the treasury function in terms of:
	— Objectives
	— Policies
	— Organisation chart
	— Responsibilities
2.4	Note the treasury's involvement in the following other areas:
	— Project finance
	— Leasing
	— Country risk analysis
	— Taxation
	— Acquisitions
	— Credit taken
	— Credit given
	— Inventory levels
	— Pension funds
	— Insurance
	— Asset renewal

3	Cash management					
3.1	ANALYSIS OF WORKING CAPITAL	Currency (£ equivalent)				
		A	B	C	D	Total
	Cash Debtors Stocks Other (specify)					
	TOTAL CURRENT ASSETS					
	Creditors Overdraft Tax Dividends Other (specify)					
	TOTAL CURRENT LIABILITIES					
	NET WORKING CAPITAL					

3.2 ANALYSIS OF CURRENT CASH COLLECTION AND DISBURSEMENT METHODS

	Collections	Disbursements
Method Cheques Bank transfers Direct debits Standing orders Cash BACS Automated cash management systems Netting/pooling systems		

4	Use of banking services					
	Note the following detail on major bank accounts managed:					
	BANK/ BRANCH	TYPE OF A/C	CURRENCY	PURPOSE	MANAGED BY★	COMMENT
	★Subsidiary or central treasury?					

5	Funds management					
5.1	Funding analysis	Currency (£ equivalent)				
		A	B	C	D	Total
	Surplus balances • maximum • minimum • average period • average yield Short-term financing • maximum • minimum • average period • average cost					
5.2	Note major methods used to invest short-term surpluses/finance short-term dificits					

6	Currency management					
6.1	Foreign exchange transactions	Currency				
		A	B	C	D	E
	Period .... **SPOT** Value of purchases Number of transactions Average per transaction					
	Value of sales Number of transactions Average per transaction					
	FORWARD Value of purchases Number of transactions Average per transaction					
	Value of sales Number of transactions Average per transaction					

Review questions for existing controls

Treasury controls checklist (sample questions*)

1   Controls of treasury department

    1.1   Are there clearly defined policies and objectives?

    1.2   Has the organisation clearly defined objectives and policies with respect to the treasury function?

    1.3   Has the organisation clearly defined objectives and policies for hedging?

    1.4   Has the board imposed authority limits and controls on treasury exposure?

    1.5   Is the adherence to these limits properly monitored?

2   Cash management

    Working capital

    2.1   Are there specified policies for the level of debtor days and is this monitored?

    2.2   Are the organisation's credit terms critically reviewed at regular intervals with marketing personnel?

    2.3   Is credit control adequate?

    2.4   Are there procedures to monitor all cash collection delays?

    2.5   Are there specified policies for the level of creditor days and is this monitored?

    2.6   Are there specified policies for the level of days of stock held and is this monitored? Cash disbursements and collections

    2.7   Is adequate authorisation required to open new bank accounts?

    2.8   Are two signatures required for disbursements over a specified level?

    2.9   Are there procedures to ensure all disbursements are properly recorded and processed?

    2.10 Is there an adequate system for monitoring expected receipts? Are there adequate procedures for chasing overdue receipts?

    2.11 Are there procedures to ensure that all receipts are properly recorded and processed?

    2.12 Are there procedures to ensure that all cash receipts are banked promptly?

    2.13 Are all bank accounts reconciled on a regular basis and the reconciliation reviewed by a senior official?

3   Use of banking services

   3.1   Are bank services reviewed?

   3.2   Are there procedures for ensuring adequate worldwide banking facilities and other financial services for group companies?

   3.3   Are procedures in 3.2 formally controlled?

4   Funds management

   4.1   Are there formalised regular and consistent procedures for identifying cash deficits and surpluses by currency?

   4.2   Are there formally defined authority limits?

   4.3   Are there counterparty limits?

   4.4   Is there a reliable forecasting base for identifying cash surpluses and deficits by currency?

   4.5   Is there regular identification of the range of investment and financing options?

   4.6   Does treasury contribute to the identification, evaluation and monitoring of long-term investments?

   4.7   Are there procedures to ensure policies are communicated to subsidiaries?

   4.8   Is there adequate segregation of duties in investment and financing transacting?

   4.9   Are financing and investment transactions adequately authorised?

   4.10   Are all transactions properly recorded on a transaction slip with sufficient details to enable processing without further reference to the dealer?

   4.11   Are there adequate procedures to ensure the complete and accurate processing of all transactions?

5   Interest rate exposure

   5.1   Is there a formal process for identification and control of interest rate exposure?

   5.2   Is consideration given to the use of new hedging techniques?

6   Exchange rate exposure

   6.1   Is a formalised exposure plan prepared on a regular basis?

   6.2   Are there procedures to ensure policy is communicated to executives charged with the responsibility of identifying and managing group exposure?

   6.3   Are there defined limits for the extent exposure is permitted to vary from zero by currency and by time?

   6.4   Is observance of these limits monitored, and monitored by senior personnel?

   6.5   Have the administrative and procedural arrangements been formally defined and established for exposure management?

7   Currency management

   7.1   Are administrative procedures and policies adequately defined?

   7.2   Is there adequate segregation of duties in foreign exchange transacting?

7.3 Is access to the dealing room limited to authorised personnel only?

7.4 Are there adequate procedures to ensure the complete and accurate processing of all transactions, eg dual level input controls, or reconciliation of dealers' manual position records to accounting records?

7.5 Are there procedures which allow senior management to monitor the activities of the dealers to ensure that they are 'dealing' within the prescribed strategy?

7.6 Are there adequate controls in the reconciliations department to ensure that funds are received in the correct account on the correct day?

7.7 Are revaluations of foreign exchange positions properly carried out?

7.8 Are the results of treasury activities properly reported to senior management?

7.9 Are the results of treasury activities properly evaluated?

8   Information needs and reporting

8.1 How reliable are cashflow forecasts?

8.2 Are sources/external forecasts regularly reviewed and evaluated?

This checklist is purely for illustrative purposes, showing only a sample of the questions that would be included in a complete version.

Checklist of controls needed in an EFT system

Controls essential to a secure system

(1)   Strong logical access controls which enforce segregation of duties within the user staff:

    a   Individual passwords and user IDs not global for particular functions or the company

    b   Easily changeable passwords by company staff

    c   Non-display of passwords

    d   Forced changing of passwords after a specified period

    e   Recording of all security violations for follow-up

    f   Screen 'lock out' after three invalid access attempts with central re-enabling

    g   Prevention of log-off before successful access to the system (to prevent multiple access attempts)

    h   Prevention of immediate re-use of 'changed' passwords (ie changing once and immediately changing back to the original password)

    i   Screen time out facility after 'x' period of inactivity

    j   Minimum length password

(2)   Adequate authorisation procedures

    a   Dual release of all payments requiring at least two people

    b   Non-display of authorisation codes

    c   Sophisticated release codes such as test keys (ie not easily guessed)

(3)   Prevention of message amendment after input

    a   Formal cancellation of messages at authorisation/release stage rather than amendment

(4)   Sufficient detail for authorisation

    a   Full screen display for authorisation including all payment details

    b   Re-input of key fields as part of authorisation procedure such as value (there fields should be displayed blank on the screen before re-input)

(5)   Full audit trail

    a   System produced full audit trail which cannot be cancelled

    b   Acknowledgement messages provided by the bank

    c   Full reporting of all non-transaction items such as alterations to the masterfile directory of beneficiaries.

Controls that are important and desirable but not essential

(1)   Pre-defined directory of payment beneficiaries held by the bank (this is only possible when the number of beneficiaries is small and relatively stable)

(2)   Value limits, variable by beneficiary

(3)   System display of date and time of last user ID usage for checking by user to ensure that there has been no unauthorised use

(4)   System not available outside pre-defined hours

(5)   Encryption (encoding) of messages

(6)   Dual test key compilation

(7)   Cumulative transfer limits (ie the sum of payments to a set beneficiary cannot be greater than £x in a given period

(8)   Terminal authentication hardcoded, ie stored physically to prevent changing (suitable back-up would however have to be considered).

Additional control considerations associated with micro based systems

(1)   System on dedicated micro not a Local Area Network (LAN) so as to prevent unauthorised access via another terminal in the network (backup will however have to be considered)

(2)   Protection of software, eg no compiler on the system. This would ensure that only programmers could make program changes

(3)   Formalised start and end-of-day procedures forced by the system including:

    a   Printing of full audit trail

    b   Taking of back-up copies of stored data

(4)   Prevention of access via the micro operating system, ie no way of bypassing the normal access controls

(5)   Holding of key fields in encrypted format, eg passwords.

CHAPTER 8

Treasury performance measurement

Treasury activities are becoming increasingly complex and treasurers are being called upon to make important decisions in the face of market uncertainty. However, numerous market research studies have shown that corporate treasurers are reluctant to introduce performance measurement techniques on their treasury activities.

This appears to be a surprising attitude for the treasurer to adopt as the production of, say, a monthly treasury management reporting package for senior management, which incorporates performance measures, would help to ensure that the quality of treasury decisions is recognised. However, many treasurers prefer to hide their light under a basket, but why? One possible, and often voiced explanation, is that treasurers fear that risk vs return decisions made while being the optimal decisions for the information available at the time, could prove in retrospect to have been less suitable and that the quality of treasury decisions would be undervalued.

However, every treasury function should be subjected to performance measurement techniques, and it is imperative that members of management understand the nature of the treasury decisions and activities reported, and the assumptions and inherent imperfections of the performance measurement techniques chosen.

This chapter begins by discussing what is meant by performance measurement and then considers the steps required in implementing a performance measurement system ('system' may refer to either manual or computerised tasks). The reporting of performance measures is then discussed, and is followed by a case study set of performance measures. This chapter ends with some 'key action points' for the corporate treasurer and/or finance director.

What is meant by performance measurement?

This chapter adopts a wide definition of performance measurement. Treasury performance measurement could be defined as quantifiable and unquantifiable attempts to assess the extent to which corporate treasury management activity is conducted in accordance with the management criteria of the company. The three elements of this definition are discussed below:

- The quantifiable or unquantifiable nature of treasury performance. As will be discussed later in this chapter, there are inherent difficulties in measuring treasury performance, many of which stem from attempts to measure opportunity gains and losses of treasury action. The assessment of a treasury's performance is a subjective area, and human judgement must be applied even to quantifiable measures
- The scope of corporate treasury management activity. Treasury performance measures are applicable at various levels in the corporate treasury department. For the purposes of this chapter, performance measures range from the assessment of treasury decisions taken by the corporate treasurer to control checks on treasury staff who contract treasury transactions

Various 'viewpoints' of treasury performance are illustrated in Figure 8.1, which shows ways in which treasury performance may be analysed. The analysis must consider the extent to which factors are controllable or uncontrollable by the treasury function.

Figure 8.1: Performance measurement viewpoints

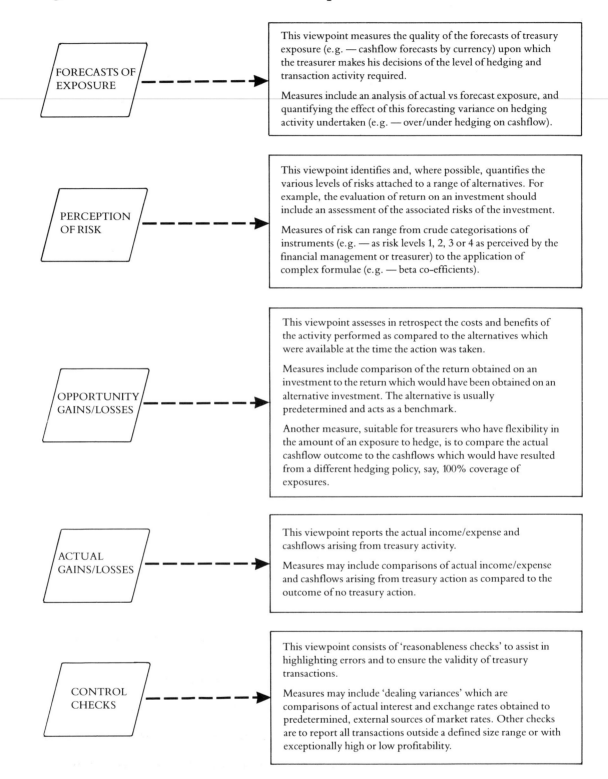

• The need to ensure that treasury performance is in accordance with the management criteria of the company. Later in this chapter we discuss the importance of ensuring that treasury performance measures relate to the objectives and responsibilities of the treasury function.

There is no standard set of performance measures to suit all corporate treasuries. The measurement techniques chosen must aim to report to management the extent to which the treasury is acting in accordance with the criteria set down by management.

For example, two treasuries with similar levels of interest exposure to manage may both have an objective to minimise short-term finance costs. If the policy of the management of one company is to maintain a 50% or more hedge against interest rate exposure, whereas the other company's management insists upon a 100% hedge, then the two companies will require different performance measures to reflect the different levels of treasury responsibility.

Implementation of performance measures

Figure 8.2 illustrates the steps involved in selecting and implementing a treasury performance reporting system. No two treasuries are identical, and the systems must be carefully chosen to suit the particular treasury function under review. Performance measurement reporting should be integral to a company's treasury reporting system. Performance measurements should be designed to be produced readily from the treasury's records where possible, almost as a by-product to recording the transactions.

Analyse the treasury activities

The first step is to analyse the treasury activities of the department. Different treasury activities have different objectives, scopes and procedures and therefore require different measures of their effectiveness. In the illustration, we have identified seven activities of a treasury function; however, often a treasury department will have other 'non-treasury' activities.

Current status of each treasury activity

The next step is to determine/assess the current status of each treasury activity identified. In doing this, there are three categories of information required:

- **Objectives and scope.** The performance of a treasury activity must be judged in light of the objectives of that activity and the scope of and constraints on the treasury's responsibilities. For example, if the treasurer is required as an objective to justify his costs and the existence of a centralised treasury, then his performance measurement will be different to the treasurer who operates as a provider of information to group companies and who is not required to justify a profit or return, but is just required to maintain a cost budget each year. Figure 8.2 illustrates the information required in order to identify the objectives and scope
- **Reasons for measuring performance.** There are a variety of potential motives in measuring treasury performance; ranging from the assessment of the quality of treasury decisions, to strengthening control; to enabling the reallocation of treasury costs to the company's profit centres. For example, a treasurer may be measuring performance in order to judge his own competence. Alternatively, he may be submitting the results to a higher authority responsible for paying his bonus based on that performance, or the treasurer may measure performance in order to justify the existence of a central treasury which services decentralised operating groups
- **Problems of measurement.** Treasury performance is notoriously difficult to measure; not least because it is often an attempt to measure an 'opportunity' gain or loss. Also, the assessment of 'risk' is fundamental to treasury decision-making, and risk is difficult to quantify.

For example, in order to measure the performance of an investment management programme, it is desirable to compare the actual investment yield to an independent 'benchmark' investment yield. The problem lies in calculating the standard investment yield. Here there is a range of complexity in the standards. At the least complex end of the continuum the performance measure can be a required rate of yield or return. At the more complex end, it can be a calculated weighted average of a certain range of investments matched to a particular risk profile over a specific period of time in a specific currency.

Also, if the assumptions underlying performance measures are not fully understood, then incorrect conclusions may result. However, these difficulties should not be used as an excuse to avoid implementing performance measures. It is better to have imperfect measures than no measures at all, although it is imperative that the imperfections are clearly understood to prevent misinterpretation of the results.

Figure 8.2: Implementation of a treasury performance measurement system

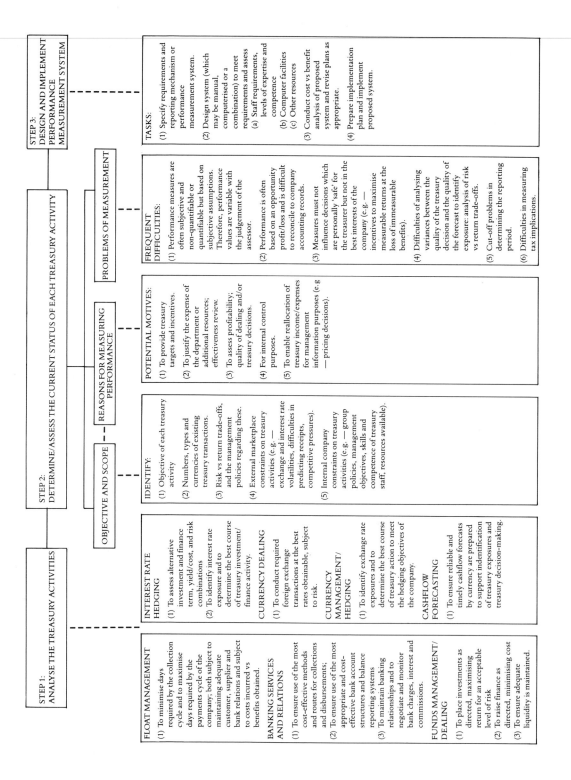

98

Design and implementation

The final boxes shown in Figure 8.2 outline the tasks required in designing and implementing a treasury performance measurement system. These tasks include the specification, design, cost/benefit evaluation and implementation of the system, which may be computerised, manual or a combination.

The performance measurement system should be produced readily by the treasury reporting system. For example, to trace a forward contract transaction through a system the procedure would be as follows. When the forward contract is executed the details would be entered on a deal slip. The deal slip would then form input to a transaction log for forward contracts which in turn would be aggregated over a chosen period, say a month, to form a management report of the forward contracts. Ideally that report, which should go to management, would have an indicator of performance which could be produced by the input to the forward exchange contract reports. For example, the comparison of the forward exchange contract rate actually dealt with a predetermined, externally obtained rate.

Performance reporting

There are three ways in which treasury performance should be reported:

- On a daily, weekly and as required basis to the corporate treasurer. These reports show in some detail both the competence of treasury dealing (for example, via a 'dealing variance' of rates obtained vs the mid-market rate of the day), and the quality of treasury management decisions (for example, the opportunity gain or loss of the action taken vs an alternative action). These reports aid the treasurer in the day-to-day management of the corporate treasury function
- On a monthly basis to senior management. A monthly treasury management reporting package, aimed at providing aggregated information of treasury performance, should be regularly prepared for senior management. This reporting package aids the senior management in controlling the treasury function, and is the reporting mechanism which treasurers seem most reluctant to introduce. An example of the performance measures included in a monthly treasury management reporting package is given in Figure 8.3
- On an exception basis to the treasurer and/or senior management as appropriate.

Treasury performance measures should be continually monitored, usually on a daily basis; and whenever measures are noted which are outside a predetermined range (whether favourable or unfavourable measures) these should be automatically reported to the corporate treasurer and/or senior management as appropriate.

Case study: examples of performance measures

The treasury performance measures of a company must be related to the objectives of the treasury department (for example, whether the treasury department is a profit centre or cost centre); and the policies and constraints on the treasury function (for example, the degree to which speculation is encouraged or discouraged by management). Therefore, there is no standard set of performance measures which is suitable for all treasuries.

Every treasury function should document, as part of a treasury operations manual, the performance measures chosen for application to its treasury activities. In addition to this, there would be detailed instructions for the recording, calculation and reporting of the performance measures.

As an example, a treasury department has the overall guidelines of firstly, minimising risk by covering exposures with low level risk hedging transactions as soon as the exposures are confidently forecast; and secondly, maximising the return/minimising the cost of treasury activity. This treasury department will have specific objectives which can be measured for each part of the treasury management process.

The objectives of this treasury department relating to float management are to minimise float time in the collection cycle and maximise reverse float time in the payment cycle. In order to measure the treasury performance in float management, the treasurer should measure bank float delays and monitor them on a regular basis. He should also monitor total float time as a measure of his success in influencing procedures throughout the organisation.

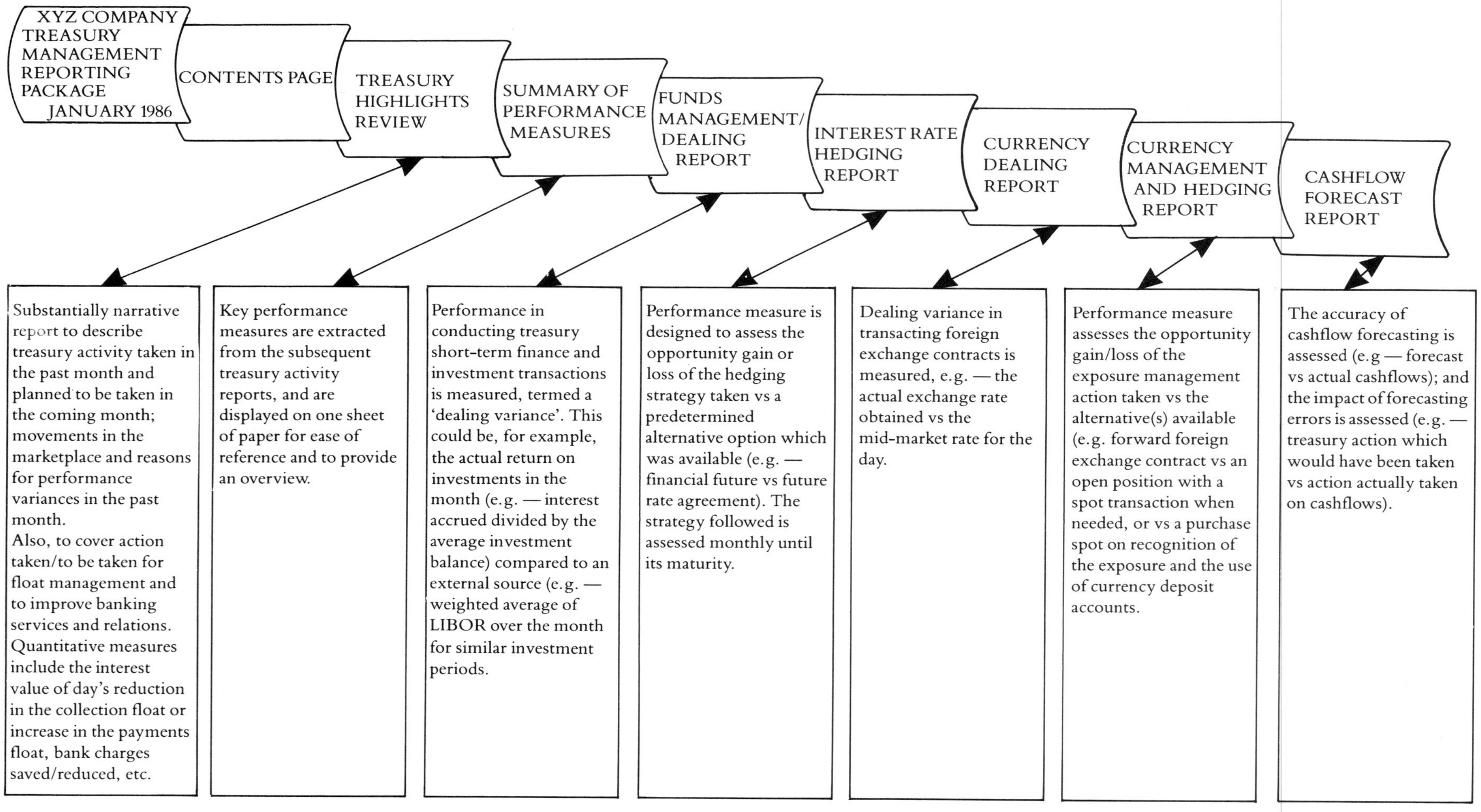

Figure 8.3: Example: Performance measures included in a monthly treasury management reporting package

Tabs:
- XYZ COMPANY TREASURY MANAGEMENT REPORTING PACKAGE JANUARY 1986
- CONTENTS PAGE
- TREASURY HIGHLIGHTS REVIEW
- SUMMARY OF PERFORMANCE MEASURES
- FUNDS MANAGEMENT/DEALING REPORT
- INTEREST RATE HEDGING REPORT
- CURRENCY DEALING REPORT
- CURRENCY MANAGEMENT AND HEDGING REPORT
- CASHFLOW FORECAST REPORT

Substantially narrative report to describe treasury activity taken in the past month and planned to be taken in the coming month; movements in the marketplace and reasons for performance variances in the past month.
Also, to cover action taken/to be taken for float management and to improve banking services and relations. Quantitative measures include the interest value of day's reduction in the collection float or increase in the payments float, bank charges saved/reduced, etc.

Key performance measures are extracted from the subsequent treasury activity reports, and are displayed on one sheet of paper for ease of reference and to provide an overview.

Performance in conducting treasury short-term finance and investment transactions is measured, termed a 'dealing variance'. This could be, for example, the actual return on investments in the month (e.g. — interest accrued divided by the average investment balance) compared to an external source (e.g. — weighted average of LIBOR over the month for similar investment periods).

Performance measure is designed to assess the opportunity gain or loss of the hedging strategy taken vs a predetermined alternative option which was available (e.g. — financial future vs future rate agreement). The strategy followed is assessed monthly until its maturity.

Dealing variance in transacting foreign exchange contracts is measured, e.g. — the actual exchange rate obtained vs the mid-market rate for the day.

Performance measure assesses the opportunity gain/loss of the exposure management action taken vs the alternative(s) available (e.g. forward foreign exchange contract vs an open position with a spot transaction when needed, or vs a purchase spot on recognition of the exposure and the use of currency deposit accounts.

The accuracy of cashflow forecasting is assessed (e.g. — forecast vs actual cashflows); and the impact of forecasting errors is assessed (e.g. — treasury action which would have been taken vs action actually taken on cashflows).

100

For the currency hedging process there are two measures of performance. Firstly, the actual currency cashflows can be compared to the cashflow forecast to establish the accuracy of the forecasting process; secondly, the treasury department should determine a measure of its own hedging performance.

Key action points for the corporate treasurer/finance director

The key action points for the corporate treasurer and/or the finance director are as follows:

- There should be performance measurement techniques linked to the objectives and policies of each treasury activity of a company.
- The procedures associated with the performance measurement techniques chosen should be documented in detail in a treasury operations manual.
- The underlying assumptions and inherent limitations of the treasury performance measures reported must be clearly understood by members of management who receive the reports.

In conclusion, the performance of a treasury function should not be exempt from measurement, whereas operating units are rigorously assessed. However, there are inherent difficulties in measuring treasury activity and different concepts of 'profit' and 'loss'. These must be appreciated in interpreting treasury performance results.

CHAPTER 9

Banking relations

The transactions of the treasury function rely heavily on sound banking relations. Banks increasingly regard the sum of their transactions with corporate clients as 'relationships', rather than on an individual transactional basis. This stems partly from changes in competitive and market conditions and partly from a realisation that it is beneficial for both the bank and its corporate client to view their business in global terms.

Advances in communication networks make it possible for both banks and their corporate clients to have available the most current data on their worldwide business. Information can be input into the communication system anywhere in the world so that the company or the bank has immediate knowledge of any change in the business relationship which has occurred. This is not just 'information for information's sake' there are several reasons why this type of data is important not the least of which is the increasing concern on the part of both companies and banks over their exposure levels to other entities. This chapter deals with the concept of 'relationship banking' from the viewpoint of both banks and their corporate clients, discusses the information which a company should provide to its principal banks and shows how a company can conduct an evaluation of its banking relationships.

A banker's view of banking relations

A decline in the profitability of certain types of banking business (most notably, term lending to prime corporate clients) has led banks to view their business in terms of the profitability of the overall corporate relationship rather than on a transactional basis. In this way it may be worthwhile for a bank to undertake low margin lending as a means of furthering a corporate relationship and thereby opening up other potentially profitable areas of business. Another factor which has pushed banks towards relationship banking is that they find it difficult to calculate their own costs and cannot accurately price individual transactions for their customers. The different approaches which banks adopt to relationship and transactional banking are illustrated in Table 9.1.

Table 9.1 - Relationship banking or transaction banking?

Category	Relationship Banking	Transaction Banking
Objective	● Profitability of total customer relationship	● Profitability of individual transaction
Strategy	● Increase business with existing customers	● Create new business
	● Cross-selling of all banking products and services	● Selling individual products and services
Marketing	● Emphasis on matching customer's needs and bank's products	● Emphasis on knowledge of bank's products
Information	● Knowledge of customer built up over a period of time	● Individual customers assessed by credit committee

Relationship banking enables a bank to obtain an overview of its exposure to each corporate client, rather than viewing the business on a transaction by transaction basis. Banks are now concerned, not only with the breakdown of their exposure by client, but also by country and industry risk. All this information can be obtained from the banking relationship data base. Within the bank, there will be at least one 'account officer' or 'relationship manager' who will be responsible for monitoring and developing the worldwide relationship between the bank and the individual corporate client.

A bank which has a strong relationship with a corporate client will build up a considerable knowledge of the business, results and plans of that company. This information is of significant value when the bank is preparing its own business plans and it can be useful in product development efforts. Most importantly for the corporate client, better information should enable the bank to provide a better service.

A treasurer's view of banking relations

For a company, the collection of information on its worldwide relationships with its bankers may be partly a reaction to the data which bank relationship managers are able to present. However, recent financial difficulties in a number of well known banks have shown that there are sound business reasons for a company to have detailed information on its exposure to each of its banks. A bank with which a company has a significant relationship can be expected to offer a much better general service than a bank which is used only for occasional transactions.

A relationship bank can usually provide advice and information on a range of economic and banking matters without placing any obligation on the company to do business. In territories where banking services are in short supply, a bank may give preference to a relationship customer with which it knows it is also doing business in more profitable parts of the world.

What should a company expect from its banking relations? These expectations might include:

- A member of the bank's staff (the relationship manager) to have overall responsibility for the relationship
- The relationship manager should have the authority to commit the bank to a reasonable level of transactions without continual reference to a higher authority
- The relationship manager to be backed up by specialists with industry, product or territorial knowledge
- Fast and effective responses to requests for information or transactions
- The submission of relevant business proposals to the company (eg interest swaps or acquisitions)
- Continuity in relationship managers or at least efficient handovers of responsibility
- An understanding of the company's full banking requirements.

A sound banking relationship should exist at different levels within the company whereby senior executives, treasurers and treasury staff have contact at the equivalent level within the bank. A rapport and degree of trust can be built up with a relationship bank over a period of time which will be beneficial to both the company and the bank.

The development of relationships between personnel from both the bank and the company will enable casual, as well as more formal, exchanges of views between the company and its bank.

There is no optimum number of banking relationships which a company should have; the number will depend upon the size of the company, the nature of its business and the international spread of its operations. Most companies have a lead clearing bank in their country of domicile and an investment bank to handle any capital market activities. Overseas operations may have their own banking relations with banks which are specialists in the financial markets of the country in question. To some extent, the number of banking relationships which a company has may be a historical issue; if the company has grown by acquisition it will have 'inherited' a number of banking relationships along the way.

Information requirements of the bank

A treasurer must be prepared for regular communication with his principal bankers to provide them with information on company strategy, market trends and any anticipated problems. It is in the interests of the company to keep its bankers informed, as a well briefed banker is able to present relevant and interesting ideas.

It is important for a company to recognise that where a bank has established a significant exposure to one company, it is reasonable for that bank to ask detailed questions on the progress of the company. In addition to this, the company should volunteer to its banks, information which might materially affect either its credit standing or the future of its business. If the bank is a party to such important information, then the bank and company may be able to work out joint solutions to problems which will safeguard both their interests.

A major relationship bank can expect to receive information about its client company as and when this information becomes available. The company should provide its bank with the following:

- Annual reports and interim and preliminary announcements
- All press releases
- Copies of any other relevant published data which may not be generally available, for example, articles about the company in specialised trade publications.

It is in the interests of the company to keep its relationship managers briefed on the progress of the company as this enables the bank to provide a better service.

Many corporate clients arrange a formal review of their banking relationships with a small number of leading banks. These reviews are generally conducted annually and enable a useful exchange of views which benefits both the company and the bank. The treasury department should have an internal discussion before such a meeting to identify any changes or improvements in service which they feel would be desirable.

It may also be useful for the bank and the company to agree and circulate an agenda for discussion ahead of the meeting. The initial part of the meeting would take the form of a description by the company of its current position. A major relationship bank can expect to be briefed on the following points:

- The expected future funding requirements of the company and guidelines on the type of funding instruments in which the company is interested
- The company's own assessment of its position in the economic cycle
- The manufacturing capabilities of the company existing at present, and future plans for expansion or rationalisation. In the case of a service company, an evaluation of the human resources and a description of future plans
- The political scene as it affects the company involving, for example, industrial relations, regional development plans and possible future legislation
- The position of major suppliers or customers of the company
- The acquisition and disposal policy of the company with approximate time horizons for future plans
- The management structure of the company with provision of organisation charts and the opportunity to meet key management personnel
- The overall financial strategy of the company with an indication of the expected time horizon for the achievement of goals
- The marketing policy in terms of market sector and geographic location, new product development and an analysis of the major competitors
- The possible effects of current and future technological change on both the company and its competitors.

The treasurer should expect the bank representatives to raise questions about the information which has been given at the meeting. The meeting should then move from general to specific topics and the second phase would be an assessment by the company of how it sees its relationship with the bank. The company should inform each bank of the following:

- Its strengths and weaknesses
- Services with a high error rate or those priced non-competitively
- Those changes required in operating procedures and cost levels
- The allocation of operating business anticipated in the ensuing year
- Anticipated borrowing, investment and balance levels.

The meeting should develop into a discussion of the relationship in which the bank and the company jointly agree how problems can be resolved and how their business may progress for the coming year. The company should take account of certain guidelines in this discussion. These are:

- The market place provides the ultimate guide for price
- All discussions should be based on the total service in question; compensation provided by other divisions, affiliates or subsidiaries should be taken into account
- Specialised services should be evaluated in isolation. Normally clear cost/benefit analyses can be made of these services on a stand-alone basis
- Balance based compensation should be avoided. The bank's rate of return applied to compute balance/fee tradeoffs is normally higher than corporate opportunity rates. It is at least worthwhile the company calculating exactly what the costs of this are likely to be
- Increases in ad valorem charge levels should be resisted since charges already provide the bank with a natural hedge against inflation
- Ad valorem/unit cost tradeoffs should be based on an 'average' company transaction size and the actual comparative costs should be calculated
- The allocation of profitable business should be used as a lever to reduce other costs or to improve the service which the bank is providing in other areas.

All the points raised and topics discussed at this meeting should be recorded in a set of notes which can either be agreed between the company and the bank or held within the company. Once finalised, these notes can be circulated to all interested parties within the company to provide a permanent record of the meeting and to form a basis for discussion the following year. Points raised during the meeting may then be checked to ensure that any necessary action is taken.

How can a company evaluate its banks?

Companies need to have a means to evaluate their banks when necessary. This may take the form of a periodic review of all banking business to ensure that the company is obtaining the optimum service in each category; or it may be a one-off review done, for example, when the company wishes to enter a new area of banking business and has to decide which bank to use.

In order to conduct such an evaluation, the company must define which present or future banking needs can be met by each bank and then judge how well these services can be executed. All the banking services which the company uses must be taken into account. Possible banking services to be reviewed in a bank evaluation might include the following:

- Current accounts
- Deposits
- Short-term loans
- Long-term loans/acquisition finance
- Foreign exchange
- Options/swaps/forward money agreements
- Financial futures
- Acceptance credit facilities
- Trade finance
- Pension fund management
- Netting/pooling arrangements
- Automatic funds transfer/information systems.

In some cases companies are adopting the formal approach of circulating Invitations to Tender (ITTs) either for new banking business or for a thorough review of their existing banking relationships. These are detailed descriptions of the company's requirements listing all known constraints which will apply. The company will request a reply to the ITT by a specific date and on that date, the company will begin to evaluate the replies.

ITTs can be circulated for all types of banking business from the funding of acquisitions to the establishment of a commercial paper programme. The type of business put out to tender will influence the range of banks approached as banks will be chosen on the basis of strength in the particular service required.

An additional service that is becoming more important in differentiating between banks is the degree and quality of advisory assistance that is provided. This service may come directly from banking officers or from specialised support groups within the bank. Advisory services span the whole area of financial concerns from foreign exchange rate forecasts to the investment of pension funds. Historically, most advisory services have been provided only by merchant, investment, or private banks. Increasingly, however, commercial banks are developing similar capabilities and provide useful economic and other information often in published form.

Having established what each bank can provide, a judgement on the quality of each bank's services must be made. Comparison, however subjective, must be made if the company is to determine which banks to employ in the absence of cost as a consideration. Criteria which could be used for evaluation are the frequency of errors, the speed with which errors are rectified once they have been brought to the bank's attention and the calibre of advisory services.

Once the company has identified those banks it prefers based on quality, it should then consider the costs of the services provided. The evaluation of quality is a subjective process, whereas the analysis of bank costs is more quantitative. In general, banks seek income either directly from commissions, spreads and fees, or indirectly through value dating, balance requirements and so on. A company can view costs either as comparative costs or as absolute cost levels.

When considering comparative costs, the treasurer should recognise that the price structures of the world's banking systems are variable. The most restrictive systems are those where some kind of cartel agreement applies to the costing structure. With the increasing focus on bank services and costs, most systems operate on an intermediate structure of standard price levels with some scope for negotiation. Some banking systems operate on the basis of negotiation alone. Countries falling within this category are characterised by relatively unstructured banking systems where clearing processes are diverse and rather unsophisticated, and thin money markets exist. Funds managers who are more conversant with sophisticated and structural financial markets often find it difficult to adjust to the numerous direct and indirect costs associated with most transactions in such a system. However, even in countries where relatively strong cartel systems exist (for example, Norway), several costs are negotiable.

Comparisons can be made even more complex when costs are influenced by compensating balances. Not only may individual costs vary but also the interest rate applied to balances to calculate balance equivalents may differ. Under these circumstances, companies must calculate balance equivalents for each service to use for comparative purposes. Once costs have been phased on a comparable basis, banks can be ranked in cost order.

Before making cost/quality tradeoffs and thus determining their banking relationships, companies should consider absolute costs levels. This is a far more difficult analysis but must be attempted if rational tradeoffs are to be made. For this analysis, companies should attempt to define precisely how much they compensate their banks. This compensation takes the following forms:

Commissions: These are amounts earned on specific transactions and bear little resemblance to the bank's cost on most activities. Even when highly automated transfer systems are installed, it is doubtful whether cheque or transfer levies in many countries cover bank operating costs.

Spreads: Banks earn a margin on loan, deposit and foreign exchange business and companies can calculate fairly accurately what compensations their banks earn. Precise levels will depend on several factors such as the nature of the market place and the type of borrowing.

Fees: Compensation from fee payments can only be considered once the underlying service and costs are identified. There are many different types of fee but two extreme examples are financing commitment fees and fees levied for advisory work. In the former situation, a case can be made that most of the fee is compensation as it is paid to ensure availability, but in the second area, payment for advisory services, the fee is far more subjective. In terms of assessing compensation, a company must determine whether the fee paid would fully cover the cost of the professionals which the bank assigned to the service and their support staff.

Value dates: To establish bank compensation, companies must differentiate between clearing time and bank value days. Once bank days are identified for each service, the associated compensation may be estimated by multiplying the related volume by the bank's opportunity rate. The identification of bank days is crucial in determining how far a company can expect to reduce value dating.

Compensating balances: Compensation on fixed balance requirements can be approximated by the bank's opportunity rate (for example, a reference rate) for demand loans. Unlike current account balances, no allowance need be made for the variability of balance levels.

By computing bank compensation, and hence the profitability of an account, companies are in a better position to negotiate improved terms. For example, the one-day value taken by European banks on all money transfer receipts and payments can be eliminated if a company can demonstrate that a sufficient level of profitable business is channelled to the bank. Thus managers can reduce total bank costs by identifying and channelling attractive business to those banks where the added compensation yields the greatest benefit.

The cost based ranking should be compared to quality based preferences. It is important to recognise that no bank can offer the best rate and lowest charges at all times and the company must select relationship banks according to their performance on business which the company regards as being of paramount importance.

Once calculated, the final rankings should be compared to the business passed to each bank and it may be apparent that some realignment is necessary. The results of analysis are essential to rational decision-making, but decisions on banking relationships cannot be made by analysis alone. The relationship between a company and a bank, and particularly between a treasurer and a relationship manager, should be a partnership where both sides consider the needs of the other. The personal element of the relationship is important and if the treasury department cannot work effectively with the relationship manager of a particular bank, then that bank may miss the chance of doing business.

Key action points

The key action points that arise from this chapter are as follows:

- Identify a full list of banking requirements.
- Assess the strengths and weaknesses of existing banks to meet these requirements.
- Hold formal evaluation meetings with bankers and raise specific issues at that meeting.
- Consider whether some areas of business or parts of the world have either an unreasonably high or low coverage by banks.
- Do not allow new banking relations to start unless there is a sound commercial reason for this.
- Be prepared to provide lead banks with information about the company and to answer their questions.
- Where new banking relations are likely to develop a formalised review process through an ITT should be undertaken.

Bibliography

Basic Handbook of Foreign Exchange Risk
Euromoney Publications

Composite Currencies
Euromoney Publications

Corporate Currency Risk
JA Donaldson, Financial Times Business Information Limited, 1980

Corporate Funding
JA Donaldson, Financial Times Business Information Limited, 1983

Countertrade
Euromoney Publications

Currency Fluctuation
David Wainman, Woodhead-Faulkner, 1976

Currency Management
Richard Lassen, Woodhead-Faulkner, 1982

Currency Risk
Euromoney Publications

Currency Risk Management
Alfred Kenyon, John Wiley & Sons, 1981

Dealing Room Design
Paull Robathan, Oyez International Business Communications Limited, 1985

Electronic Treasury Management
Peter Gallant, Woodhead-Faulkner, 1985

Financial Futures
Euromoney Publications

Forfaiting
Euromoney Publications

Foreign Exchange and the Corporate Treasurer
John Heywood, Adam and Charles Black, 1979

Foreign Exchange and Money Markets
Heinz Riehl & Rita M Rodriguez, McGraw Hill, 1983

Foreign Exchange Dealers Handbook
Raymond Coninx, Woodhead-Faulkner, 1986

Foreign Exchange Handbook
Steven Bell & Brian Kettell, Graham & Trotman, 1983

Foreign Exchange Management
McRae & Walker, Prentice-Hall, 1980

Foreign Exchange Rates: Theory and Practice
M & Morrell Lesseps, Henley Centre for Forecasting, 1977

Foreign Exchange Risk
AR Prindl, John Wiley & Sons, 1976

Foreign Exchange Today
Raymond Coninx, Woodhead-Faulkner, 1978

Foreign Exchange Trading Techniques
DR Mandich, American Bankers Association, 1976

A Guide to Financial Times Statistics
Financial Times Business Information Limited, 1985

The International Money Market
G Dufey & I Kiddy, Prentice-Hall, 1978

The Management of Foreign Exchange Risk (second edition)
Euromoney publications

Letters of Credit
Euromoney Publications

The Money Market
Marcia Stigum, Dow Jones-Irwin, 1983

Practical Liquidity Management
Michael Tennent, Gower Press, 1976

Swap Financing Techniques
Euromoney Publications

Treasury Management
John Giannotti & Richard Smith, John Wiley & Sons, 1981

Treasury Management in the UK
Edward Davis & Paul Collier, Association of Corporate Treasurers, 1982

A World Guide to Exchange Control Regulations
Euromoney Publications

Glossary of terms

Aggregate risk

The exposure of one counterparty to another up to the value date of a contract. Exposure is therefore limited to the fluctuation between the rate on which the deal has been agreed and the market rate at the time the second counterparty ceases to trade.

American option

An option that can be exercised at any time prior to expiration.

Arbitrage

The process of buying a currency in one market and selling it simultaneously in another market at a higher price. Arbitrage may also be applied to interest rate differentials.

At-the-money

An option where the exercise price of the option is equal to the market price of the underlying asset.

Base currency

A single unit of one currency which is used as the base on which another currency's value is expressed. For example: in a quotation of £1 = $2.0 sterling is the base currency. See quote currency.

Big figures

See quote currency.

Blotters

The work sheets on which a dealer maintains a record of the deals agreed and the resulting open position.

Broken dates

The forward dates for which market prices are not readily available, for example one month and 10 days. Broken date quotes are based upon interpolation between fixed date prices.

Broker

An intermediary acting between two or more banks in order to provide an efficient and ready interbank market. Brokers are unable to take their own positions.

Buyer

The purchaser of an option, either a call option or a put option.

Calendar spread

A spread involving the simultaneous sale of an option with a nearby expiration date and the purchase of an option with a more deferred expiration date. Both options have the same exercise price.

Call option

An option giving the buyer the right but not the obligation to purchase the underlying asset at a fixed exercise price at or before expiration.

Cash management

Action taken to conserve cash resources.

Cash mobilisation

A series of techniques to ensure the efficient movement or transfer of cash.

Cash pooling

The process of concentrating available funds for investing and financing purposes in order to minimise idle balances.

Certificate of deposits

A bearer security issued by banks and other financial institutions which is especially common among US banks and institutions.

CHAPS

Clearing house automated payments system. The UK bank clearing system operating with same day value.

CHIPS

Clearing house interbank payments system. The New York bank clearing system operating with same-day value.

Class of options

All call options or put options on the same underlying asset.

Clean risk

The exposure of one counterparty to another on the value date of a deal. This is the risk that one counterparty to a deal may have received funds but is unable to pay the exchanged currency. Theoretically only the counterparty paying funds in the Far East of Europe should suffer clean risk due to the time delay of receipt of US dollars. Clean risk was defined as a result of the Herstatt Bank collapse in 1974.

Closing purchase transaction

The purchase of an option identical in exercise price and expiration date to an option originally sold. This is used to liquidate an open option position.

Combination

A position created either by purchasing a put or a call option, or writing a put and a call option, on the same underlying asset.

Currency management

The process of co-ordinating and executing dealing transactions within an overall strategy.

Counterparty

The organisation, usually a bank, with whom exchange deals are agreed.

Covered option

A written option is covered if it is matched by an opposing cash or futures position in the underlying asset, or by an opposing option position of specific characteristics.

Dealer

An employee responsible for making and agreeing the individual deals with each counterparty; usually within one area of trading eg: foreign exchange or money markets. In a large treasury each area could be sub-divided into different currencies.

Del credere risk

See clean risk.

Delta

A measure of the relative volatility of an option price to the price of the underlying asset.

Direct quotations

An exchange rate quotation in which the local currency is the quote currency and the other currency is the base currency. For example, in West Germany a direct quotation is $1 = DM2.

Discounts

See premium and discounts.

EFTPOS

Electronic Funds Transfer at Point of Sale. EFTPOS uses a customer's individual debit card to transfer funds from his bank account to the retailer's via a computer link.

Electronic funds transfer

Movement of funds from one bank account to another via a computer link.

Euromarket

An international market for the investment of currencies (Eurocurrencies) outside their country of origin and therefore free from government interference.

European Monetary System (EMS)

An agreement between some members of the EEC to reduce fluctuations in their cross rates of exchange. Initiated 13 March 1979.

European option

A call or put option that can be exercised only on the expiration date.

Exercise

The action taken by the holder of an option contract to exercise his right. When a call is exercised, the holder acquires the underlying asset at the option exercise price. When a put is exercised, the holder sells the underlying asset at the option exercise price.

Exercise price

The price at which the option holder may buy or sell the underlying asset, as defined in the option contract.

Expiration date

The date after which an option can no longer be exercised.

Exposure management

The process of minimising the risk of changes in interest and/or exchange rates by using various techniques which are both internal and external to the company.

Fair value

The option value derived from a mathematical option valuation model.

Fixed dates

The forward dates for which market prices are readily available, normally in whole months ie one, two, three, and six months. See broken dates.

Float

The time delay associated with each stage of the cash collection cycle from order entry to receipt of good value for funds in the banking system.

Forfaiting

The process of an exporter selling bills of promissory notes to a financier where all credit and financial risks are undertaken by the financier (or the forfaiteur).

Forward rate

A rate at which an agreement may be made to exchange one currency for another at a specified future date, which is usually any date more than five working days from the transaction date. The difference from the spot exchange rate is termed a premium or a discount. See outright deal.

Funds management

The process of investing cash surpluses and financing cash requirements based on amount and term.

Fungible

An option which is transportable between exchanges.

Gamma

The second alternative of the option price relative to the stock price. It indicates the stability of the delta.

Hedge

The protection of a specific option position against price risk by buying or selling offsetting positions.

Hedge ratio

The delta of an option derived from an option valuation model. It indicates the proportions in which options and the underlying stock should be combined to give a position in variance to price movements.

Hedging

The process of minimising exposure to currency and interest rate risk by using techniques such as netting, matching or forward contracts etc.

Horizontal spread

Same as a calendar spread.

Implied volatility

The value of asset price volatility that will equate the market price of an option with the fair value of an option.

Indirect quote

An exchange rate quotation in which the local currency is the base currency and the other currency is valued as an expression of the local currency. Eg: in West Germany an indirect quotation is DM1 = $0.5. See base currency and quote currency.

In-the-money

An option is said to be in-the-money if it has intrinsic value. A call is in-the-money if the asset price is above the exercise price; a put is in-the-money if the asset price is below the exercise price.

Intrinsic value

The amount of profit that would be realised if the option were immediately exercised.

Investment term

The period of time between the contract and the maturity (value) dates of a placing.

Leading and lagging

The process of adjusting the timing of receipts and payments to facilitate a specific treasury strategy.

LIBOR

The London Interbank Offered Rate. A recognised basis to calculate a floating interest rate, usually agreed as LIBOR plus X %.

Local authority bill

A bearer document issued by UK local authorities for terms up to one year.

Local authority deposits

A non negotiable, fixed term deposit with a UK local authority.

Long

The position which is established by the purchase of an asset or option if there is no offsetting position.

Margin

The sum of money which must be deposited with the clearing house or broker by the writer of options to protect the clearing house against his non-performance.

Matching

The process of offsetting total receipts and payments in like currencies with respect to amount and timing.

Naked writing

Writing a call or a put option on an underlying asset which is not owned by the writer.

Netting

The process of offsetting intragroup transactions to reduce transfer values. Netting can be either a bilateral or a multilateral process.

Opening transaction

The purchase or writing of a put or call option which establishes a new position.

Option

The right but not the obligation to buy or sell a specific quantity of a specific asset at a fixed price at or before a future date.

Option premium

The price of an option - the sum of money which the option buyer pays and the option writer receives for the rights granted by the option.

Option spread

A position involving the purchase and sale of call or put options on the same underlying asset but with different striking prices and/or expiration dates.

Out-of-the-money

An option that has no intrinsic value. For a call the exercise price is above the asset price; for a put the exercise price is below the asset price.

Outright (forward) deal

The exchange of one currency for another at a future date rather than at the spot date. The exchange rate will be the spot rate adjusted by the forward premium or discount for the forward period and not, therefore, the market expectation of the spot rate as at that date.

Overnight

See short dates.

Pips and points

See quote currency.

Positions

The net balance of the purchase and sale foreign exchange transactions agreed by a dealer. A position is therefore the amount of the exposure to price changes. Positions are usually expressed in dollar amounts and subject to strict limitations.

Premium and discounts

The differential between a spot exchange rate and forward exchange rate which is based upon the difference between the Eurocurrency interest rates over the period for the two currencies.

Put option

An option which gives the buyer the right but not the obligation to sell the underlying asset at a fixed price at or before the expiration date.

Quote currency

The rate of one currency expressed against the base of another, eg: in a quotation of £1 = $2.0, $ is the quote currency. The amount of the quote currency will change upon market conditions and expectations. When the base currency becomes stronger or the quote currency becomes weaker the rate will rise, conversely when the base currency becomes weaker or the quote currency becomes stronger the rate will fall.

Rates are usually quoted to 5 digits, eg: £1/$ at 1.4830. The last two digits are termed the 'pips' or the 'points', the middle digit is 'the big figure', the first three together are 'the big figures'.

Reverse float

The time delay associated with each stage of the cash payment cycle, from initiation of payment to loss of value.

Risk management

The process of reducing the impact of risk related events. Strategic risk management is the quantification of cashflow effects of, for example, a major disaster. Operational risk management relates to the insurance process.

Seller

Equivalent to an option writer.

Series

All options of the same class having the same exercise price and expiration date.

Short

The position created by the sale of an asset or option if there is no offsetting position.

Short dates

The maturity dates up to seven working days from the transaction date, including overnight (today until tomorrow), tom/next (tomorrow to the day after), spot/next (spot value date to the day after), spot-a-week (spot value date to one calendar week later).

Snake

An agreement, now superseded by the EMS, between several European countries to limit fluctuations in the cross rates of exchange.

Speculation

A series of deals made independently of any underlying commercial transaction, usually instigated in order to generate additional profits. Speculation is the opposite of hedging.

Spot-a-week

See short dates.

Spot deal

The exchange of one currency for another, one of which is dollars, at the agreed current rate of exchange, normally for payment and receipt of the funds in two working days.

Spot/next

See short dates.

Spread

The difference between the buying and the selling prices (or the borrowing and the lending prices) at which a transaction may take place. The spread represents part of the profit element for the counterparty.

Straddle

A combination of a put and a call option on the same underlying asset, each with the same exercise price and expiration date.

Strike price

Same as exercise price.

Swap

A pair of transactions, in which there is a simultaneous purchase and sale of an agreed amount of one currency for another at two different dates. In a spot/forward swap, the two dates are the spot date and one in the future. In a forward/forward swap both dates are in the future.

SWIFT

Society for Worldwide Interbank Financial Telecommunication - a non profit making organisation owned by banks to enable reliable and independent worldwide communications.

Term

The period of investment and the period for which funds may be committed to other parties.

Theta

The rate of change of the option price with time. It indicates the rate of loss in value of the option as the expiry date approaches.

Time value

The amount by which an option's premium exceeds its intrinsic value.

Tom/next

See short dates.

Transaction date

The calendar date on which a transaction is agreed.

Uncovered option

Same as naked option.

Value date

The maturity date on which funds are exchanged or repaid. Most spot exchange contracts have a value date two working days after the transaction date. See also short dates, fixed dates and broken dates.

Volatility

A measure of the amount by which an asset price is expected to fluctuate over a given period of time. Normally measured by the annual standard deviation of the natural logarithm of daily price changes.

Writer

The seller of a call or a put option in connection with an opening transaction.

PW publications
—a selection of publications available from Price Waterhouse in London

Investing in the UK
1 Tax Implications for German Companies
2 Tax Implications for US Corporations
3 Tax Implications for Japanese Companies

Doing Business Guides (in individual countries)

Futures and Options Accounting and Administration

Minicomputers and Control

Microcomputers — their use and misuse in your business

Evlauation and Testing of EDP Controls

An Accountant's Guide to the Oil Industry

UK Taxation on the Profits from North Sea Oil

Management Buy-Outs

Employment Abroad
A Guide to the Tax Problems

International Banking Series
VAT in London
VAT in Germany
VAT in Sweden
VAT in Dublin

Corporate Taxes
A Worldwide Summary

Individual Taxes
A Worldwide Summary

The Unlisted Securities Market

Treasury Management Services

The World's Major Stock Exchanges
— Listing Requirements

Merger & Acquisition Service
Acquiring A Company — An Information Checklist

A Glossary of Insolvency Terms

A Banker's Guide to Survival

Creditors' Rights in England and Wales

Services to the Securities Industry in a Changing Financial World

International Tax Review

Indirect Tax News

Corporate Finance Advisory Services for Business Wishing to Raise Money

Price Waterhouse Services to Banks and Financial Institutions

UK Taxation for Overseas Nationals

Similar publications are available at other Price Waterhouse offices

PW in the financial centres

Argentina — Buenos Aires
Casilla de Correo Central 896
1000 Buenos Aires
Telephone: (1) 35-3005
Telex: 21777
(Robert S Taylor)

Australia — Sydney
50 Bridge Street (GPO Box 4177)
Sydney NSW 2001
Telephone: (2) 238-1533
Telex: 21798
(David P Craig)

Austria — Vienna
IPW Interaudit Prüfungs — und
Wirtschaftsberatungs — GesmbH
Traungasse 12
A-1030 Vienna
Telephone: (222) 73-24-59
Telex: 136805 (IPWVI A)
(Peter Buchbinder)

Bahamas — Nassau
ED Sassoon Building (PO Box N-3910)
Parliament Street
Nassau
Telephone: (809) 322-8543
Telex: NS 297-20-146
(Trevor Gorman)

Bahrain — Manama
4th Floor, Unitag House (PO Box 26403)
Government Road
Manama
Telephone: 233266
Telex: 8964 (PWBAH BN)
(Tam Basunia)

Belgium — Brussels
Rue Ravenstein 60, Bte 7,
B-1000 Brussels
Telephone: (2) 513-92-80
Telex: 22716 PWCOB
(Paul Pauwels)

Brazil — São Paulo
Edificio Independencia (Caixa Postal 1978)
Rua General Jardim 36
01051 São Paulo SP
Telephone: (11) 259-2511
Telex: (011) 21864
(Irineu de Mula)

Canada — Toronto
Toronto-Dominion Tower (PO Box 51)
Toronto, Ontario M5K 1G1
Telephone: (416) 863-1133
Telex: 06-524111
(Bob Mitchell)

Cayman Islands — Grand Cayman, BWI
First Home Tower (PO Box 258)
British-American Centre
Jennett Street
George Town
Telephone: (809) 949 2944
Telex: CP 293-4-329
(Richard Harris)

China — People's Republic of
1015 Beijing Hotel
Beijing
Telephone: 507766 Ext 1015
Telex: 22423 SHELB CN
(Margaret Jack)

France — Paris
Blanchard Chauveau & Associates SA
18 Place Henri Bergson
F-75008 Paris
Telephone: (1) 294-16-16
Telex: 641873
(Jean-Pierre Tauss)

Germany, Federal Republic of
— Frankfurt
Myliusstrasse 33-37
Postfach 17-04-64
D-6000 Frankfurt 1
Telephone: (611) 7147-0
Telex: 4-189-120 (PWCD)
(Jermyn Brooks)

Hong Kong
Prince's Building
22nd Floor (PO Box 690)
Telephone: 5-222111
Telex: 73751 (PW HK)
(Frank Mullens)

Ireland, Republic of — Dublin
Gardner House
Wilton Place
Dublin 2
Telephone: 605199
Telex: 24349
(John B Dillon)

Italy — Milan
Corso Europa, 2
20122 Milan
Telephone: (39-2) 77851
Telex: 334173 (PWCOMI I)
(Alberto Giussani)

Italy — Rome
Via Aniene 30
00198 Rome
Telephone: (6) 844-01-51
Telex: 611526 (PWCORO I)
(Emilio Palma)

Japan — Tokyo
Aoyama Buildings, 7th Floor
(CPO Box 797)
2-3 Kita-Aoyama 1-chome
Minato-ku
Tokyo 100-91
Telephone: 404-9351
Telex: 24355
(Shibayama Koichi)

GD- Luxembourg
20 Avenue Pasteur
2310 Luxembourg
Telephone: (325) 23562
Telex: 1231 (PWCO LU)
(William Bannerman)

Malaysia — Kuala Lumpur
Chartered Bank Building
(PO Box 10192)
2 Jalan Ampang
Telephone: 203833
Telex: MA 30018 (PW)
(R Arshad Uda)

Mexico — Mexico City
Reforma 243, 7° Piso
(Apartado Postal 1403)
06500-Mexico DF
Telephone: 533-10-00
Telex: 01772579 (GVPWME)
(A Ferreira)

Netherlands — The Hague
Koninginnegracht 8 (PO Box 30439)
2514 AA The Hague
Telephone: (70) 924631
Telex: 31315
(David Winter)

Philippines — Manila
Rufino Building, 8th Floor (PO Box 2288)
6784 Ayala Avenue
Makati, Metro Manila
Telephone: 86-59-00
Telex: 22370 (RCA)
(Corazon de la Paz)

Saudi Arabia, Riyadh
International Accounting Associates
(PO Box 41711) Al-Math'har Building
Riyadh — 11531
Telephone: (1) 476-1236
Telex: 200788 (PRICEW SJ)
(James Schneider)

Singapore
1 Science Centre Road 08-00
Unity House
Telephone: 5612222
Telex: RS 23039
(David Mason)

Spain — Madrid
Princesa 3
Madrid 28008
Telephone: (1) 241-96-04
Telex: 42164 (PWCO E)
(Paul Menmuir)

Sweden — Stockholm
Brunkebergstorg 2 (PO Box 1612)
S-1186 Stockholm
Telephone: (8) 22-82-20
Telex: 11694 (PWCO S)
(Ronald Hathorn)

Switzerland — Zürich
Börsenstrasse 26
8022 Zürich
Telephone: (1) 211-2-52
Telex: 812000 (PWZH)
(Reto Weber)

United Arab Emirates — Abu Dhabi
1st Floor (PO Box 3646)
Ahmed Obeidley Building
Istiklal Street
Telephone: 334138
Telex: 24178 (PWCO AD)
(David Hurst)

United Arab Emirates — Dubai
1302 Pearl Building (PO Box 11987)
The Creek
Deira
Telephone: 284206
Telex: 47471 (PWCO EM)
(Peter Farrar)

United Kingdom — London
Southwark Towers
32 London Bridge Street
London SE1 9SY
Telephone: (1) 407-8989
Telex: 884657
(Paul Reyniers)

United Kingdom — Birmingham
Livery House, 169 Edmund Street
Birmingham B3 2JB
Telephone: (21) 236-5011
Telex: 338689
(George Carter)

United Kingdom — Edinburgh
8 Melville Crescent
Edinburgh EH3 7LZ
Telephone: (31) 225-4242
Telex: 727434 (PWEDIN G)
(Ian Adam)

United States of America — New York
153 East 53rd Street
New York 10022
Telephone: (212) 371-2000
Telex: 1-26142
(Len Lundegren)

United States of America — Chicago
200 East Randolph Drive
Chicago, Illinois 60601
Telephone: (312) 565-1500
Telex: 2-54018
(Bill Linnenbringer)

United States of America — Houston
1200 Milam, Suite 2900
Houston, Texas 77002
Telephone: (713) 654-4100
Telex: 701646
(George Powell)

United States of America — San Francisco
555 California Street
San Francisco, California 94104
Telephone: (415) 393-8500
Telex: 753821
(James Jensen)

Venezuela — Caracas
Edificio Del Rio
7th Floor
Avenida Cafetal, Chuao
Caracas 1010-A
Telephone: 91-81-11
Telex: PRWAT CY 23366
(Mary Sanchez)
Mail Address:
Espineira Shildony Asociades
c/o Jet International — M347
PO Box 020010
Miama, Florida 33102-0010

International Treasury Management Team
PW, London
1 London Bridge
London SE1 9UL
Telephone: (1) 407-8989
Telex: 931709/934716
Telecopier: 403 5265

The PW central team servicing international
treasury management is:
- Mark Austen and Paul Reyniers
  (Consultancy)
- Nigel Buchanan and Richard Kilsby
  (Audit)
- Mike Maskall and Nick Hughes
  (Tax)